To Shonaig
Christmas 1989
All my love
Roger
xx

WHAT NEXT?

WHAT NEXT?

by

George Davies

with Jessica Davies

CENTURY
LONDON SYDNEY AUCKLAND JOHANNESBERG

Furst published in Great Britain in 1989 by Century
An imprint of Century Hutchinson Ltd
Brookmount House, 62-65 Chandos Place, Covent Garden, London WC2N 4NW

Century Hutchinson Australia (Pty) Ltd
89-91 Albion Street, Surry Hills, New South Wales 2010, Australia

Century Hutchinson New Zealand Ltd
PO Box 40-086, 32-34 View Road, Glenfield, Auckland 10, New Zealand

Century Hutchinson South Africa (Pty) Ltd
PO Box 337, Berglei 2012, South Africa

Set in Linotronic Ehrhardt by
SX Composing Ltd, Rayleigh, Essex
Printed and bound in Great Britain by
Mackays of Chatham

British Library Cataloguing in Publication data
Davies George
  What next?
  1. Great Britain. Retailing. Biographies
  I. Title
  658.8'7'00924

ISBN 0-7126-3493-2

To Liz, for all the reasons we both know.

Thanks for all the help and support to Liz and I, particularly
from our family – Mother, sister Pam, Irena and Stan and
daughters Melanie, Emma and Alex and even little Lucia, and
to all my very dear friends, including Andrew and Frances,
Anne, Kevin, Chris and Sandra, Geoffrey, Nick, Mark, Bob,
Hugh and Sheila, Tony and Irene, Roger and Ann, Ian, Denis,
Leslie, Gerry and Jill, David and Caroline, Chris and Liz,
Brian and Janet, Linda, and David who I will always miss.

CONTENTS

PROLOGUE

Friday 12 February 1982

9:00 a.m. in Newport. It was an awful morning, one of those black, wet, wintry mornings and I couldn't find Next. I parked my car in a random side street, and wandered until I rounded a corner and saw our illuminated sign shining through the grey drizzle. I felt a tight knot of nerves in the pit of my stomach, and I knew I couldn't go into the store yet. I couldn't bear to stand there waiting for the first customer to arrive, like some anxious father-to-be, pacing the hospital corridor while his wife gives birth. I decided that I would have to go for a walk and return later. I don't remember where I went, but it can't have been far, for at 9.45 I was back outside the Next store.

'How much have you taken so far?' I asked the manageress, in as casual a tone as I could muster, noticing as I spoke that there were some six or seven customers milling about the small shop. '£1,400,' came the reply. The knot in my stomach began to loosen. Upstairs I found a phone, and I dialled the Harrogate store. The phone their end was on the shop floor, and the hubbub I could hear down the line was enough to convince me that the response there was good as well. Coventry, Burton-on-Trent, Eastbourne and Douglas, on the Isle of Man – the news with each phone call was the same. In Slough, I learnt, the girls from Wallis had come across the road to place their orders the previous evening! By now elated, I knew that Next's first seven stores had taken off. That evening, back at my hotel in Bath, the figures for our first day's trading began to come through. Alan MacNeil, our Sales Director, had predicted £4,000 for the day, but it was soon evident that we had achieved 2½ times that level of sales.

The Next revolution had started as it would continue. Between August 1982 and January 1988, our profits would soar from £3.9m through to £92.4m. We became the most talked about retailing phenomenon of the 80s, and we were described variously in the press as 'the fabulously successful fashion chain' (the *Daily Express*), 'a lesson to British industry' (*The Guardian*), and 'the most exciting and fastest growing retail group in the high street' (*The Sunday Times*). We were credited with transforming not only the High Street, but the fashion sense of the British shopper too, and scores of other retailers attempted to imitate our style. We could do no wrong.

As the man who had originally been recruited by J. Hepworth and Son (the Leeds men's wear group) to develop and launch the Next ladies' wear concept, and who ultimately rose to become Chairman and Chief Executive of a £1 billion empire, I too could do no wrong. I was the darling of the City, and of both fashion and business press, and I was the recipient of a string of awards.

But then late one evening in December of 1988, the Next that my team and I had built during the past eight years was snatched from me in a sudden boardroom coup. 'The man who made Next,' said the *Daily Telegraph*, 'walked away from it all yesterday. George Davies and his wife Liz, who has worked alongside him in creating one of the biggest success stories in British retailing, have, said the group, "ceased their executive functions".'

The day of that report, I was due to receive a marketing award for the Next Directory from the British Direct Marketing Association. I was to make a speech, but of course I never did. What had happened to change my fortunes so dramatically, and why? Had those eight years of endeavour been totally wasted? And most importantly, without Next, where did my future lie?

1

THE COMPETITIVE INSTINCT

Good people

I've always believed that it's when people hurt you badly that you move forward, and my whole life has been about that. Life is about going on, and not giving up when you're put down. If you hold on to bitterness and look only for revenge, you aren't going to get anywhere. We all suffer blows, and my story is a story of fighting back whenever people and circumstances have turned against me.

One of the first times I felt the pain of rejection was when I was blackballed from a Liverpool football club. I'd returned home after a brief spell at Birmingham University, where I'd been playing semi-professionally with Bangor City. The Liverpool Ramblers was an amateur club, but when two of my friends who were members suggested I join, it seemed a good idea.

I thought no more of it until some weeks later when I was told that somebody in the club had blackballed me, and that I was therefore debarred from membership. I was puzzled, and thought that maybe I'd done something wrong. But I hadn't counted on the club's conventions. It had been founded in the 1900s for ex-Etonians and

Harrovians. Subsequently it had opened its doors to old boys of other soccer-playing public schools. And by the time I came along, members included people who'd been to rugby-playing public schools. There were no ex-grammar schoolboys like me, however.

The incident hurt me, but I didn't let it get to me – there was no point. Two years later one of my oldest friends, Dave Appleton, asked me to have another go at joining the club. I'd been playing with one of the best amateur clubs around – Marine – but I'd broken my leg, and was looking for a way of getting back into the game. This time nobody blackballed me and within a matter of weeks I was on the first team. Funnily enough I actually ended up as Liverpool Ramblers' longest-serving captain and some of the best times of my life were spent in the little hut they called a pavilion, socializing after the matches.

In a way I even began to see why they had rejected me at the outset – it was all about maintaining standards, and that's why it was a difficult club to get into. You have to keep these things in perspective. And actually, the guy who blackballed me is now a very good friend; he wrote me a lovely letter when I was fired from Next.

For a greater part of my teens I suffered from a sense of inferiority. When I was 14, we moved from Netherton (a small country village), to Crosby, a nice middle-class suburb of Liverpool. At the local golf club I met a new crowd of friends, who were mostly public schoolboys. My social life began to revolve around the West Lancashire golf club and these new friends. I hadn't really thought about class before, but now for the first time I began to look at myself and wish that I lived in a nicer house, that my parents were wealthier, that they could afford to send me away to school. Things have changed now, and we're more of a meritocracy, but in those days your chance of success was far greater if you'd been to public school – we all knew that.

What made me aware of being 'inferior' was the occasional party that I wasn't invited to, and to which only the people with the 'right' backgrounds went, and the way in which some of my friends' parents treated me. My lack of height was something else that made me self-conscious. But all these things prepare you for later life, and harden your resolve to make a success of yourself. Having some self-doubts can actually be quite beneficial because they can make you more determined in the long run.

I don't think I can have inherited my ambitious streak from my father, also called George, for he was a very contented man who never felt the need to prove anything to anybody. He left school at 16 and worked for the same family-owned bakery and pie factory for more than forty years. There was a great wisdom about him, and a sense of satisfaction with his lot. In the week of his death at 74 I got closer to him than ever before. I witnessed his strength in the face of immense pain. 'I'm fighting, George, by God I'm fighting,' he told me that day he died. He was never a showy, openly ambitious man, but he had great inner strength.

My mother, Mary, was the belle of the village when my father met her and she's still a very good-looking woman. Her father was a farmer, and the family lived in an old country village outside Liverpool called Sefton. My father used to go that way as one of his company's pie factories was in the village. I'll never forget that factory – it was one of my childhood treats to go on Sundays with my father to make pies and then put them into the lovely old ovens.

A great dressmaker, was my mother, and even during and after the last war, when clothes and fabrics were so scarce, she managed to wear some very fine outfits. Perhaps that's where my interest in fashion started. She's the sort of woman who is always turned out smartly, and who never comes downstairs before she's put on her make-up. While my father provided the levelling influence in our household, my mother was the dynamo of the marriage.

She was highly ambitious. While my sister always got on especially well with my father, I was closer to my mother. She would protect me even when I was in the wrong and still can't bear to hear me criticised. She wanted the best for me, and I've always been aware of not wanting to let her down in any way.

In the past, I tended to believe that I took after her more than my father, but now I can see both of my parents in me.

I was born on 29 October 1941, and christened George William. George was something of a family name: not only was my father a George, but so was my maternal grandfather, and my sister was christened Pamela Georgina. Then there was my mother's brother, Uncle

George. He was a bit of a rogue and liked to live the high life. There was a glamour about Uncle George, as he came and went in one or other of his fast cars, and he always seemed rather mysterious to me. I never really knew what he did for a living, except that he was forever buying and selling things. I adored him.

Those early days were wonderful times. Netherton is now built up and I wouldn't recognize it any longer, but then it was nothing more than two rows of houses surrounded by fields. Those were the War years, but our lives were hardly affected. I remember the wail of the air raid siren, and a large iron kitchen table under which we would all hide. My father was a Sergeant in the Catering Corps, stationed in Germany. I have a memory of him writing to say he was coming home, and promising that he would bring me a train set. I was about 3 at the time, and I was quite convinced my train set would come complete with real little people, who would walk out of the compartments when the train pulled in. I was quite surprised when they didn't. I enjoyed the space, the animals and the freedom. My friends and I used to go into the country-side for whole days, hunting for birds' eggs to add to our collections.

I recall especially the attitude of the country people – they were such nice, good people. My maternal grandfather, the farmer, was a very quiet and loving man with gnarled fingers and weatherbeaten skin that was always brown. He was a great man of the earth, and ploughed his fields with a team of horses. Once, when one of the horses bit off his ear, Grandfather simply stuck it back in place with brown sticking paper and carried on working. He lived until the age of 95.

I was always keen on sport, and that was probably what carried me through my mediocre school results. My sister Pamela, who is eighteen months older than I, always did very well at school. She was never below the top five in her class, whereas I tended to stay somewhere in the middle. The school always described me as 'a tryer', although I don't think I did try that hard, but because I was good at soccer and reasonably polite, they seemed quite happy with me.

Even at the age of 6 I was determined not to be left behind. I was a very slow reader and while the rest of my class had progressed to Book Three, I was still stuck on Book One. Then one day, our teacher left, and a replacement arrived. She went round the class, and asked each one of us which book we were on. I saw it as my chance to catch up, and told her I was on Book Three. I suppose I must then have pushed myself very hard, because my reading improved dramatically, and the teacher never caught me out.

I sat the 11-plus, and passed it, much to everyone's surprise. My sister had been the certainty, whereas I'd just been a good soccer player. Pamela had won a local authority scholarship to a local public school, Merchant Taylors', and that's where my mother wanted me to go too. But I was still only 10 ½, and they weren't prepared to take me on before the age of 11. So I went to Bootle Grammar School and when, after a year, I won my place at Merchant Taylor's, I decided to stay where I was: I had made my friends and I was playing soccer, and at Merchant Taylor's they only played rugby.

Bootle Grammar School was a brilliant training ground for life, because you met every sort of person there. It was a microcosm of the real world, and it taught me how to mix with all sorts of people. There were the wealthy kids, and the respectable kids – the sons of businessmen and vicars. But there were also some really rough lads – I remember one boy carving his initials in his arm with a razor blade, and then rubbing the wound with salt so that the marks would remain. I tried to keep away from the real knife-wielding toughies. I was something of a loner, mainly because I lived out in the country while most of the other boys were from Bootle, and some of them accused me of 'speaking posh' because I didn't have a heavy Liverpudlian accent.

My mother *had* tried to rid me of *my* accent by sending me to elocution lessons, but she never completely succeeded and the intonations are still there. I started going to see Mrs Ackerley at the age of 11. She was one of those highly theatrical people who wore lots of make-up, and who would greet me with an imperious, 'Come in, my darling'. She had me doing, 'How now brown cow,' and I also remember having to recite the William Davies poem:

What is this life if, full of care,
We have no time to stand and stare.

I still find it difficult to say 'there' the way Mrs Ackerley would have liked. And in a way I'm glad, because I don't think anyone should ever be ashamed of where they come from.

Playing for England

But it was my sport, and soccer in particular, that ultimately gave me the self-confidence I lacked. Soccer was in my blood: my father had been a great sportsman, playing as an amateur at Everton in the days of Dixie Dean, the greatest soccer player of all time. Although he wasn't personally ambitious, my father pushed me very hard when it came to soccer. He was highly critical of my performance, and even if I had scored three goals in a match, he would say, 'Well George, you didn't play all that well.' At one point I asked him not to come and watch me, because I felt I couldn't play as well while he was there.

I was a fearless player, and I would go after even the most difficult ball. A lot of the other players were bigger than me, but I didn't mind. I would just throw myself into the game. I loved the camaraderie and the sense of team spirit; it's wonderful to win together, even to lose together and to travel to the games together. Team sports are terribly important, I believe, and I've found that many of the best businessmen I've known have played sport to a very high standard.

While I was in the sixth form, I was selected for Merseyside Grammar Schools. We played a series of matches, and I was picked as twelfth man of the Lancashire Schoolboys side. As luck would have it, someone fell ill, and I got on to the side for my first big match. I had a great game, and became a permanent fixture on the team.

My next break came in the shape of an invitation to attend what was called an England School Week down in Oxford. We were to have a week of intensive coaching, after which selection would be made for the England Schoolboys' side. I remember there were a lot of the so-called stars there – boys from West Ham, Arsenal and so on. The Saturday evening arrived when the selected side was to be read out. I was an inside forward, and they passed that position calling out somebody else's name. But when they got to the last position on the list, they called out, 'Outside left, George Davies.' It was a wonderful moment, I couldn't believe that I'd actually made the England side!

We went to meet the Scots at Turf Moor, which is Burnley's ground. There was a good crowd there, in their thousands, and I scored the winning goal. The next day I found I'd made the back page of the *Daily*

Express, and when I got home that evening my mother told me that Liverpool had been on the phone, and that they wanted me to go for trials. I'll never forget the day Bill Shankley, their legendary manager, came round to our house. He sat in our lounge, and said to my mother, 'George has potential.'

2

A LATE DEVELOPER

Drifting

So at the age of 18 I really hadn't decided what I was going to do in terms of a career. It seemed like a good idea to go to Liverpool for a couple of weeks of trials, but by the end of those two weeks, I knew I didn't want to take up soccer professionally. I realized that in a sense sport is no longer sport when it becomes professional. Of course there's no point in playing if you don't *try* to win, because that then belittles your opponent's victory, and no one wants to play against someone who can't be bothered. But if winning is all that matters, you quickly lose all those other elements that make sport so pleasurable.

On the other hand because I had been playing so much sport, I didn't have much time for the academic side of things, and when I reached my last year at school I decided not to apply for University – I didn't expect much from my A level results. I think the terminology they use at school is 'late developer' and in my case it meant that I was 18 years old, and didn't know what I wanted to do. Schools aren't that good at preparing you for the real world, and I looked at all the usual things – banking, insurance and so on. One of my friends had joined the Navy, and I even thought about going to Sandhurst, but in the end I found myself putting on a stiff collar and starting a job that summer at the Royal Insurance in Liverpool. They had offered me work two years before, when I was taking my O levels, so it seemed as good a place to go as any.

My starting salary was £300, with an extra £15 because I had taken A levels – £5 for each subject! I was a trainee in the North John Street branch office and I soon discovered that the work wasn't going to stretch me. In retrospect, I believe there was a lot that was good about the Royal Insurance. They were quite forward-thinking for the time and trainees would be sent on residential courses over in Hoylake, on the Wirral. I sat and passed the first part of my ACCI Association exam. My job was to check policies for legal points.

The most enjoyable part of life at the Royal Insurance was going down to the vaults where they kept all the archives, and where – if you were lucky – you might have a little session with one of the girls who worked down there. Having been very naïve and sexually unaware throughout my early teens, when I did discover women, I went crazy. During my year at the Royal Insurance I would have a different girl every two or three weeks. A lot of my friends had steady girlfriends, but I definitely didn't. In spite of that I was always very careful in my relationships with women – in those days I think people were far more cautious anyway, but with me it was also because I was frightened of letting my mother down. I knew that if I got a girl pregnant I'd never be able to face her.

Life was good. Too easy, perhaps, but good. This was the Beatles era, and at lunchtime we'd escape from work and go down to the Cavern. We'd return with sweat pouring from us, and the old boys in the office would give us stick for being late. In the evenings we'd go back to clubs like the Mardis Gras where we could jive to the Mersey City Men and Acker Bilk.

People like the Beatles were starting to dress in a different way, and they were highly influential on my fashion sense. I'd always been interested in clothes and when I was 13 I'd got my mother to buy me a double-breasted blazer from John Manners, the school outfitters, made in a lovely fine wool called barathea. Everyone else had the ordinary woolly serge blazer, but I wanted something better. Now that at the age of 18 I had some money of my own, I bought my first made-to-measure suit. Most of my friends bought theirs off-the-peg. I thought I was a real dandy. But I was always quite careful and lived within my means, and even today I won't buy anything unless I have the money to pay for it.

They were great times, but I was drifting, and I remember periods when I felt very flat. But then something happened which made me stop short and think about what my goal was in life.

Johnny Humphries had been one of my best friends at school. He was a brilliant guy who'd been the star pupil and head boy. The day he should have gone up to Oxford he died of leukaemia. During the period leading up to his death, I spent a lot of time with him. Sometimes he was fine, and a whole crowd of us would go down to the open-air swimming baths at Southport, but he was always in and out of hospital having blood transfusions. The night he died I was at a party. My memory of that time is vague – it was one of those very painful things that you tend to block out. I do remember going to see his mother, and the funeral. We were all very upset – it seemed so unfair.

I began to think about what it was all about, and where I was going. My A level results had come through and much to my surprise I'd done reasonably well. While still at school, I'd spoken to my mother about going into dentistry – it didn't require high marks. I applied for Birmingham University and got a place on the Bachelor of Dental Surgery course.

For the first time I found myself living away from home, and to begin with I was very lonely. My landlady was a Mrs Sprag, and she used to play hell with me, claiming that I was the most untidy man she had ever come across. This was probably because I took ten suits with me, and there was nowhere to hang them but on the picture rail!

I don't think that even at that point I'd learned to work properly. Inevitably, soccer had become my key interest again. I went to the freshers' trials, and got on to the Birmingham University side straight away. I then played for Birmingham County, before being selected for English Universities.

The holidays were magnificent. I was playing tennis and golf and doing very little in the way of studying which meant that when the end of the academic year came around I failed the exam.

My Mother Intervenes

I must have been disappointed, but I expect the next day I went out and played tennis again. Life was still pretty good, and I kept telling myself that I could always go back and sit the exam the following year. However, my mother told me that I couldn't play tennis for the rest of my life and that I was going to have to get a job, and the sense of dissatisfaction with the way my life was going, which had been prompted by the death of John Humphries, came to the surface again.

I wrote more or less at random to two large Merseyside companies enquiring about trainee management positions: one was Fibreglass, a subsidiary of Pilkingtons, and the other was Littlewoods. Littlewoods replied, inviting me to an interview. I went along to see them, and after giving me an IQ test they told me that they'd like to offer me a traineeship in stock control.

Part of me wasn't over-keen to knuckle down to a proper career yet, and I always remember saying to them, 'Well, I'm not sure if this is what I want to do at all.' They said that if I wanted the job, I could start that Monday. I claimed that I needed a couple of weeks to sort myself out, and they agreed. Looking back on that conversation, I can't think why they took me on at all – I wouldn't have!

So this was to be the beginning of my real working life. I had had two false starts – I had spent a year at the Royal Insurance and a year at University. When you are young you sometimes look around at your friends, panic and think, 'My God, I've wasted a year.' But one year – or even two – at that stage is irrelevant in the context of your whole life. Sometimes you need that time to work things out, and it's best not to hurry. The best things grow slowly. When my eldest daughter Melanie, who's now 22, didn't get the marks she'd wanted at A level, she came to me and asked me what she should do. I told her that it was her decision, but that I saw three options: she could go on a training course at Next, she could go and work abroad, or she could have another go at the exams. She took the last option, went to a crammer in Oxford and got excellent marks. She's just finished her degree course in Business Production at Nottingham University. So you see, that extra year wasn't wasted at all.

Up to the age of 18 I had regarded myself primarily as a sportsman. Now I would turn my competitive instincts to business.

3

BUSINESS PRACTICE

Littlewoods

I look on my career as a continuing business education, and Littlewoods was where it really started. The nine years I would spend there were to give me vital grounding and experience in retailing. There are no short cuts. They were tough times in some ways. Initially much of my work seemed like drudgery, but I soon learned that drudgery is a state of mind, and that you can influence business, even if you are working at the lowest level.

I joined Littlewoods in the October of 1962 as an ankle sock controller. It was a figures job, which involved looking at sales sheets and working out how to divide the available stock among the different stores. I had to juggle figures all day, which I quite enjoyed as I'd always been good at maths – it was just as well, for in those days there was no computer to do the work. Every other Monday we would receive a large box of paperwork which gave us the opening stock, the receipts and the closing stock for each of the shops. Our future allocations were based on this information, so we had to comb through it meticulously. I always remember the time the manager at Ashton-under-Lyme, a tiny

13

store , filled in his form incorrectly: instead of quoting his opening stock as 3 dozen pairs of socks, he wrote 300, which would have inundated the place.

Those early years on stock control taught me a valuable lesson about good and bad business practice. I learned that if you make a mistake – if you buy in 300 dozen white ankle socks, and they don't sell – you first have to mark the stock down, or give it away to Oxfam. That's the way the money goes, and that's why correct stock levels are so crucial. Many people in retail get into trouble because of their stock levels.

I set myself the task of finding better ways of controlling our stock. As I learned my trade, so I began to bring in judgement rather than simply letting the figures control me; I read between the long lists of numbers and tried to identify trends, and that's where the job began to get interesting – as I say, drudgery is a state of mind. Looking at sales histories carefully, I began to pick out local trends and patterns. In Manchester, for instance, they had Whit walks during the Whit half-term. It was a semi-religious occasion, and all the kids would be dressed in white. So, whilst normally in Manchester you might be selling 15 dozen pairs of white ankle socks a week, in the week before Whitsun, you'd get through 180 dozen.

There were different patterns all over the country – seaside towns like Blackpool, Morecambe and Margate, for instance, tended to have a longer season than elsewhere. That may seem obvious, but you'd be surprised how few people pick up on the obvious – in business I've learned that the most uncommon thing is common sense. For example, if the stock controllers had 100 dozen pairs of socks and ten shops, they'd simply send 10 dozen to each, irrespective of demand; or if the last set of figures showed that a shop had sold 2 dozen pairs, and that shop needed a further four weeks' stock, they'd just send off 8 dozen. It's simple to work to formulas like that – but it's not good business.

Stock holding is about looking *forwards*, not backwards. Most people relate to sales gone by, when in fact they should be looking at what is going to be sold *next* week, the week after that and the week after that. The work started to make me sensitive to customers: it wasn't the past figures that were controlling my stock decisions, but the customer and forecasts based on his buying patterns. While many people would have found my job boring, I began to feel that I was achieving something.

I remember going to one of my first appraisals, about six months after I'd arrived. They were complimentary about my work, but then my boss, a man called Colin Shiner, told me that I wasn't too good at expressing myself and that I tended to jumble my words. I walked out feeling bloody annoyed, but determined to improve. I knew that in business you've got to be able to communicate effectively, so I took the point on board. In later years, and especially at Next, public speaking was a regular feature of my working life and I came to enjoy it.

Colin would subsequently join me after I left Littlewoods to set up my own business, and he was one of the founding team at Next. But in those days he was the boss, and it was he whom I had to go and see about my soccer commitments, shortly after joining Littlewoods. I'd been picked to play for the England Amateur side at Sheffield, and because the match started at 6.30, I was going to have to ask to leave work at 4 p.m. I asked Colin if that would be all right and I was a bit miffed when he said no. Nonetheless, I accepted his decision and turned down the match. Little did I know that twenty-five years later at Next, I would be standing in Colin's shoes, telling one of my members of staff the same thing: Sean Kerly joined us as Trainee Buyer on Sports Equipment when we acquired Collingwoods with the Combined English Stores takeover in May 1987. He'd been picked to play in the British hockey team at the South Korea Olympics, so we knew he'd be off work for quite a while. I was a great supporter of the Olympics in those days, and had agreed his period of leave. But then he came to me saying the team needed more of his time, and he was going to have to quit work several months before the Games. Would he get his job back when he returned? I had to tell him that he ran the risk of losing it: there's amateur sport and there's professional sport, and if you're doing it virtually full time, you can't expect your employer to carry on making allowances for prolonged absences. It's not fair on the rest of the team who are left behind to pick up the pieces.

Within six months of joining Littlewoods I had my own section, with four people working under me, and I was then promoted to childrens' wear stock controller, with a staff of sixteen a year later. But I wanted something better. I'd realized soon that although there was a tremendous community atmosphere, stock controllers were definitely the second class citizens. We would sit in the middle of the buying floor, surrounded by buyers peering down on to us from their glass offices. Littlewoods always kept the responsibilities of stock controllers and buyers quite separate, and I've tended to follow that example. It gives you a balanced judgement: if a buyer likes something, he's bound to go out and buy it in quantity, but the stock controllers can then come in with their judgement, and moderate the purchase. The two disciplines complement one another.

I was given a chance to move across to buying sooner than I'd anticipated. I was stock controller on childrens' wear. It was a hot summer and there'd been a rush on short-sleeved dresses. The trouble was, we were very short of stock, because of the laziness of one of our buyers. She was pleasant enough, but she just didn't do her job. We needed the dresses, but I wasn't able to order more until the relevant buyer had selected the designs. I kept going to see her, but she did nothing about it. I'm not a great player by the rules so in the end I went off to Belfast to visit the suppliers – John Sherrard Limited. I sat down with the designer, and we put together a selection of dresses. When I got home, the buyer whose job I'd just done didn't seem at all bothered – I think she was glad someone had made the effort for her. For my part, her laziness had given me the opportunity to start developing out of stock control and into buying.

A Questioning Attitude

So two and a half years after starting at Littlewoods, I was invited to join the buying office. Normally you would have had to have been a store manager first, but my efforts had been recognized. Not that it was an easy move; having run my own show, I was now back to making the tea. As a trainee buyer, you were kicked around. There was one chap, Mr Alexander, who used to give me a specially hard time. He drilled me mercilessly, making me reel off the price of every dress in the kids' department at Marks and Spencer. His attitude changed overnight, however, when he saw me up a ladder in Ainsdale, a beach area near Southport. I'd bought a plot of land there and was building my house. Alexander saw me, and assumed I'd got a temporary job as a builder.

He was very surprised to hear the house I was building was my own – he was having one built in the same area! My troubles with him were over. But his aggressive attitude had already taught me a lot: a measure of insecurity, and a tough boss make you learn faster than anything else. We were under tremendous pressure, because everything had to be done in a strict seven-day cycle. Once the sales sheets came in for the different shops, you had to go through them, work out your repeat buys for each shop and allocate accordingly. If you didn't get that done by the Monday, you'd lost the whole week. There was always someone leaning over your shoulder, checking you were doing the job correctly, and hurrying you along. I found the pressure exciting. It's important for young people to go through a period of learning the ropes – at the moment too many people come straight from University, expecting instant promotion and big salaries. In the end they always lose out to the ones who have gone through the learning curve, experiencing what it's like to be at the bottom. Hard graft at the beginning of your career makes you a better decision-taker later on. There are very few successful people who haven't started that way.

Littlewoods had a marvellous training department, run by a man called Vic Steele. As well as learning on the job, I was sent on a series of excellent releases which taught me all about the textile industry. I remember spending weeks travelling around garment manufacturers and cloth mills. I always had questions running through my mind: I had to understand the total picture, why certain types of fabric were used for certain types of garment, and how the process had developed. A lot of people don't bother to go through that kind of logic, but I needed to know why things were done the way they were done. If you don't do that, if you don't understand the underlying principles, you can't move forward. I have been described as a visionary. That vision is built on an historical base, a detailed study of the deeper, wider patterns.

My questioning attitude was to stand me in good stead when I came to the end of my training. After two years, two written exams and an interview with the Old Man of Littlewoods himself, John Moores, and the MD, Phil Carter, who's now Chairman of Everton and was President of the Football League, I qualified as a buyer. I had been given babies' wear while still a trainee, and now I was made buyer for infants'

17

wear as well. One of the garments I introduced was called the Play-Overall; it was like a romper suit, and retailed at 21/-. It hadn't been selling as well as I'd hoped, so I began looking into its production and discovered that there was a cheaper way of making the garment, using a similar fabric. Our cloth department had provided us with a knitted fabric called piqué, but when I went down to the factory and got talking to one of the knitters, I found that the cheaper interlock fabric would do the job just as well, and that it could be produced more quickly. We managed to move the price down to 19/11d, and sales rose from £30,000 a season to £1 million. It confirmed my belief that you should never accept things if you can improve them. It also taught me how sensitive the customer is to price, a lesson I would apply over and over again at Next.

The next big area for which I was given responsibility was boys' wear, and that was when I met a chap who's still a friend today. Buying from abroad was rare in those days, particularly in kids' wear. We did have one foreign supplier on trousers, however, a Portuguese company called Maconde and on my first day in boys' wear in walked their new representative, called John Fishbourne. I remember him sitting opposite me in a little office, showing me his range and then confessing that he knew nothing about trousers. 'Well, John,' I replied, 'I've got something to tell you. I've just come from girls' wear and I know all there is to know about dresses, but nothing about trousers either. You never know, if we work at it, we might be able to learn together.'

And we did. My predecessor had had a bad experience with Maconde the previous season – the goods had arrived late, and they weren't the right ones anyway. I told John about this, explaining our side of the business to him and what we needed from our suppliers – it wasn't just a matter of buying the right garment, but it was also getting it delivered on time, in the right quality and to the right specifications. We needed, too, to be able to react to unforeseen sales patterns. This meant his people would have to hold on to extra cloth, just in case we had a boom in sales. I assured John that any leftover cloth could be used the following year anyway – grey terylene/worsted wool is timeless.

Suppliers don't like doing that sort of thing: it's complicated and – the received view is – it's risky. Of course, it's always easier not to take risks. John was a businessman, however, and he agreed to return with me to Portugal where we laid down the law together. Maconde subsequently became one of Littlewoods' largest suppliers of trousers.

The Buyer/Supplier Partnership

That's how I've always built my supply structure. I believe that the buyer/supplier relationship should be a partnership. My attitude has always been to start off by saying that we are *both* trying to sell to the customer, and that if we work together, even share some of the risks together, we have a better chance of success. If I screw you on price, the chances are you'll flog me shoddy goods next time round, which won't get either of us anywhere. The element of risk, from your point of view, arises because you're having to trust someone to keep their side of the bargain. But people with integrity will recognize each other, and that's when buyer and supplier can start building together. The strength of any retailer is in his supply structure, and if you don't have a decent supply structure you'll never win. If you do you can begin working towards that extra ingredient called vision, in which the buyer works with the supplier to design the right garment at the right time. Vision requires an extra added ingredient of flair and inspiration, but, as I said earlier, the greater part of it is solid, working practices – you need to get those right first.

At the age of 24 and beginning to apply these lessons, I was doing well. I was younger than anyone else in my position, and I was beginning to earn the respect of senior buyers. One of my coups was the matching shirt and tie. It took off to such a degree, that the mens' wear shirt buyer asked to have a look at some of my other ideas. I began travelling to the Far East, until then exclusively the province of buyers in mens' wear. I soon realized that my colleagues in mens' wear were being cocooned by the same inferior suppliers. They were not bothering to look for new people – which gave them the freedom to spend most of their trips lying in the sun. I was determined not to follow their example. I was determined to see new suppliers. Sometimes I would return from a trip empty-handed, because I'd found nothing that satisfied me. It takes tremendous strength of personality to do that when your boss has forked out the fare, but in the long run your integrity will earn you respect.

In the end I actually wrote a report saying that I thought the way we worked in Hong Kong was quite wrong. The response was nil. People often just don't want to know. They feel secure in old ways of working (a deceptive sense of security, I should say), and often they are enjoying perks that make life just too comfortable for them to think about change.

There were other things that began to frustrate me about Littlewoods, and now I began to give some serious thoughts to my long-term prospects. These considerations were given a new impetus by my marriage at the age of 23 to Anne, and the birth of our first daughter, Melanie, within the year. What I had achieved in terms of the profitability of my section that year, was not recognized at the end of year salary reviews. Everybody got the same rise, which was ridiculous, because it meant that the loafer who did nothing got the same as I. Management was copping out.

I began to look around the floor: one of my colleagues was a very nice guy – a shirt buyer – who'd been doing his job for forty years. Of course he had a good salary, his trips to Hong Kong and so forth. But I thought to myself, 'Is this all I want out of life? Do I want to look back and say, that's the sum total of my achievement?' I decided then that I might be doing all right by other people's standards, and by the standards of Littlewoods, but not by my own.

What finally did it for me, however, was the promotion of Arthur Raley. He was nice enough, but with a very smooth image that I didn't like. He knew nothing about buying, and I was told he was to train with me. Within four months he was whisked away and promoted to Group Controller. He was the boss of all the buyers, yet he had never bought. I, who had been on the courses and passed the exams and interviews, was now his subordinate. Funnily enough, he's still there today.

This sort of incident can be tremendously demotivating. In my case it prompted me to look elsewhere. I knew I had the ability, but I wasn't getting any recognition. Meanwhile, my confidence had grown immeasurably during my nine years at Littlewoods, and I found I could do things of which I hadn't thought myself capable. My brother-in-law was running a garage and in one year I sold forty cars to colleagues at

Littlewoods; then I'd thought about setting up a small building business. I also remember going up to the Lake District with my brother-in-law to look at a hotel called the Wordsworth in Grasmere with a view to buying it. I had become an avid reader of the *Financial Times*, and was enthralled by the dynamic progress of Jim Slater, of Slater Walker.

A Gap in the Market

It was, in fact, a job I was doing for Littlewoods that finally gave me the idea I needed to break away. I was chairing a working party examining how various aspects of the business might be improved. One of the areas was the Back to School mail order range. The more I looked at the market and what we were offering it, the more I realized that schoolwear was not something a large mail order company like Littlewoods could do successfully.

I'd learned that when you are analysing a market, you should always start off with the big picture and then refine it down to the detail – a lot of people dive straight into the detail, without understanding the wider context. So my first step was to discover the size of the schoolwear market. I then had to look at who was in it and what they were doing, or failing to do. It was clear that the market was large, but what was significant to me was that it had begun to change with the advent of comprehensives. Under the old system, grammar school head teachers had dictated what schoolchildren should wear, and where their parents should buy it – in other words, the school's approved outfitter, which was always very expensive. The uniform was a status symbol for the school, a mark of superiority directed at outsiders. But in the sixties with the arrival of comprehensives, the point of having a uniform changed: the new socialism now promoted equality and conformity over status. Headmasters still wanted to keep standards, but a uniform became more of a levelling device, so that rich and poor children all dressed alike. The problem was that many parents of children who would previously have gone to secondary moderns and so not need uniforms now couldn't afford the £30 or £40 it cost (even then) to buy a blazer at the school approved outfitters. Littlewoods, Marks and Spencer, and British Homestores had only continued to offer basic ranges in black and navy. The value was much better, but the lack of

21

specialization (which included other popular colours) meant that 80% of the market was still having to go to the small specialist retailer where prices were high. It was obvious that there was a niche in the market for someone who could provide the same level of service as the specialist, but who also had the techniques of the generalist to achieve volume.

I started to follow the idea through for myself. I realized that although black and navy were certainly popular, green, purple and maroon were the other basic colours. Nobody had ever tried to standardize them, however, which meant that every head teacher had an idea in their head of what 'their' green, purple or maroon was. I could see there was a huge marketing opportunity for anyone who could persuade these people to come over to a standard green or whatever, because you could then buy in bulk. They would benefit from lower prices.

Because people are very resistant to change, I had to work on persuading head teachers that there was no such thing as 'their' colour. One of the tactics I adopted was to take them out into their own playground and say, 'Now tell me which is your purple.' When you've got uniforms that have been bought over a series of years, none of the purples are going to be the same. Different batches of cloth come out different shades and clothes fade, in any case. So the colour the headmaster had had in his mind was quite different from what his pupils were actually wearing. My idea could not compromise his colour, because he'd never had that colour in the first place. We would still stock small individual items, like his tie and his badge, because the investment would be low. But the basic garment would come from our stock which we would buy in bulk – cheaply.

The next problem was how to reach all of these schools in volume without setting up a chain of shops. The answer was mail order, and I struck upon the idea of using the schools as agents. This meant that they actually distributed the catalogues to the parents, and received a commission of 5% on all sales. It was my first major marketing ploy, and it worked.

With each of these new ideas for the business, I went through a series of check points. When you're trying to break new ground as an entrepreneur your enthusiasm will tend to carry you away, and you are then in danger of making bad decisions. On the one hand, you need optimism, because without that nothing ever gets done; but on the other hand, you need to develop check points on the way to keep you in line. Each of these must be passed satisfactorily before proceeding to the next stage, just as you check a map when you're driving to an unfamiliar destiny. In addition, I would always use other people as sounding boards – mainly not business associates but my potential customers. I also spoke to John Fishbourne who would eventually invest personally in my idea, and Chris Fagan, a stock controller, who would leave Littlewoods to work for me in the venture.

The Total Look

I handed in my notice at Littlewoods in the December of 1971, and set up my own company, School Care, the following January. It was going to be a whole new learning experience for me. I was a natural marketeer, and my work had taught me about stock controlling and buying. But what did I know about warehousing? Or administration of a multi-disciplined staff? What did I know about systems? Or finance, banking, overdrafts and gearing? And what, for that matter, did I know about advertising? I was going to have to learn as I went along.

We didn't have much time – there was only six months until our launch on July 1st 1972. Buying cycles fall into natural patterns, and normally you need nine months from product development to launch, so we were already three months short. But in many ways that was good: the momentum tends to go if you take things at a slow pace.

The concept I developed for School Care in some ways foreshadowed Next. I tried to provide a 'total look' for schoolchildren (an innovation in 1971) by developing quality products of exceptional value. Another innovative thing I tried to do was to inject some fashion into the range. There were two types of blazer available for schoolboys at the time; one was the old fluffy Melton, which looked a bit like blanket cloth, the other was made out of what's called Shoddy, which was reclaimed wool collected by the rag and bone man. There was a third option, which was worsted wool, but that was very expensive. Crimplene was starting to be used in men's suits, so I developed a crimplene blazer for schoolboys as a fourth, practical and better-looking alternative. I know that nowadays people look down on crimplene and polyesters, but those fibres were coming through at that time and they became very popular, even fashionable. The blazer was fully lined, so it was warm, and it was totally washable, so it retained its smartness.

Because School Care was my first business, I did come up against problems I hadn't anticipated. We quickly realized, for instance, that because a manual index was inadequate we would have to introduce a small computer system to hold the names and addresses of our customers; the worst thing that can happen to any mail order business is not to have a reliable and comprehensive data bank. This is just one example of the many little internal things that can trip you up when you're starting business. The amount of detailed planning required is immense. You have to be prepared for everything even, in our case, knowing when your suppliers took their holidays.

One area where I knew I definitely needed help was credit. A lot of schools we were signing up weren't wealthy, and kitting a kid out for the first time was an expensive business – even at our prices it was going to come to £80 or £90 altogether. I contacted a credit company in Bradford called Provident and set up a deal with them, whereby any of my customers applying for credit could go through them. Credit wasn't freely available in those days, which meant that it didn't come cheap. Provident charged the customer in excess of 30%, as well as taking a 12% commission from me.

The launch was a tremendous success, and School Care took off fantastically well. We had 180 Lancashire schools on our books, and the orders were coming in thick and fast. I soon found that as many as 20% of our orders came with applications for credit. My team and I did as we had been instructed by Provident: they had given us a list of their area branches, and we sent each application off to its appropriate branch. After three weeks or so, we had heard nothing back from the majority of the branches, and we were beginning to get complaints from our customers. What the hell was going on?

It was a classic case of the central office in a large organization not knowing what went on at branch level. Provident had a sophisticated head office, and you would have thought they knew what they were doing, but they didn't. Head office clearly didn't realize that by their own rules every applicant for credit had to be visited personally by a Provident representative. I'd been sending dozens of applications, inundating the branch offices. Furthermore, if they decided an applicant wasn't from 'their patch', they'd simply put the paper at the bottom of the pile. Head office had also not anticipated the huge generation of business and therefore hadn't bothered to sell School Care to their branch offices; I went to one branch and was told, 'We've had these little slips through, and we don't know what we're supposed to do with thcm.' As it turned out, we generated more new business for Provident than anyone else that year.

Had I discovered the problems any later, I'd have been dead. But fortunately, the customers didn't need the goods until the beginning of the school year, so we had some time in hand. I sat down with Provident's senior management and worked out the system they'd need to deal with our business. We mapped out every street in every area so that there could be no confusion whatsoever about whose patch was whose. It required a tremendous effort from me, but I had to get my sales, so I had to do the work even though it wasn't mine to do.

The experience taught me a great deal about the credit industry and I began to see ways in which I could exploit my relationship with Provident to develop my business. They had a team of door-to-door agents who sold goods and credit. The credit side was the early form of a Barclaycard. Your cheque for, say, £50 could be spent in the shops, and you would then pay it off with interest over the weeks. The difference between that old system and what we have now, is that those agents acted as their customers' personal bank managers. Why not exploit that one-to-one relationship, and use those agents to sell products other than schoolwear? I quickly saw that most of my turnover was done during a peak three months, after which sales tailed off until the beginning of the following school year. Why not develop a fashion range which I could sell through the Provident agents during the quieter months?

We developed a ladies' wear range and produced a series of very successful mini catalogues which were taken round by the agents during the lulls in the schoolwear business. It was during one of these lulls in School Care's third year that the Provident agents decided to go on strike. I had printed my catalogues and ordered the stock, and now I was suddenly without any sales.

The money I'd raised three years previously to set up School Care had come from a number of sources: there was £50,000 of my friends' and my own money. I'd also got a company called Hollis to put a further £40,000 into the venture – they were a Blackburn-based public company involved in property and textiles. (And coincidentally they became a major supplier to Asda, who would play a significant part in my future. Life goes in circles, never in straight lines.) Hollis had introduced me to a secondary bank called Northern Commercial Trust, who'd given me an overdraft facility without security of £200,000. So from day one, my borrowings put me squarely in the hands of the bank – I was very highly geared, which basically means that I was using a lot of borrowed money. And on top of the bank's massive interest payments, which were in the region of 17%, I was having to pay out my 12% commission on all the sales that went through Provident.

Throughout our first two years we'd done phenomenally well: we'd broken even in year one, and we'd made profits of £20,000 in year two. But now, with the Provident strike, we suddenly found ourselves struggling. When we did our third year accounts, we came out with a small loss of £10,000. Northern Commercial Trust began to put pressure on us to reduce our borrowings and when they were taken over by the Dutch bank, ABN, the pressure on us became more intense. The overdraft facility was whittled down to £100,000, which meant that I had real cash flow problems. Businesses don't usually collapse because they're not making money; they collapse because of cash flow. Providing you have the money coming in to run the show, making a loss can be overcome and doesn't necessarily leave you broke. But if you're at the mercy of the bank, and they decide not to give you any money to keep the business running, you're in trouble.

I went to Hollis for support, but they weren't able to help. I understood them to be under a certain amount of pressure themselves in the property world, as well as having to finance large letters of credit on goods from the Far East, so they had their own difficulties which I appreciated. I then had the idea of approaching Provident. I explained that I was being leaned on heavily by the bank, and that if I was forced to

26

close down the business, Provident were going to lose a lot of commission. The deal I proposed was that they refund me some of their commission for that year so that I could then go into profit and thereby win back the confidence of the bank – the sum we were talking about was £80,000. Provident could see that my proposal made sense, and said at our meeting that they'd go with it. The next day, however, they phoned me with the news that they'd discussed the matter further and had changed their minds. Things then began to happen very quickly: the bank had no alternative but to appoint a receiver. The day after the receiver moved in, Provident called to say that they would, after all, lend me the money. The offer came too late.

If there is such a thing as an honourable close down, then the close down of School Care was that. The creditors didn't put us into liquidation, mainly because very few people lost money. The main losers were the original investors like my friends and myself. I'd lost in excess of £20,000, which was a lot of money by my standards. John Fishbourne, whom I'd met that first day on boys' wear in Littlewoods, lost £5,000. It was tough, but investment is a risk. John was marvellous about it. I remember him saying to me, 'If I make an investment, I write off that money the next day.' And I think you should never invest money you can't afford. I would certainly always advise the individual investor to be cautious and to spread any risk – then, unless there's a total collapse of the market, you're unlikely to lose out in the long run.

The concept I'd had was good, and had School Care been correctly financed it would have flourished. We had got over all the hurdles, but we needed cash to continue building the business. We were crucified because when the crisis came, we were too highly geared. The lack of real equity and consequent level of borrowing meant that the risk had been too great. The bank was charging us interest at 17% and as a small business that sort of rate is crippling – one or two percentage points can make the difference between profit and loss, success and failure.

It's never pleasant when things go wrong with a business, and they were hard times. But I remember thinking that I wasn't going to let it get to me. I'd been a twinge away from being a millionaire, but it hadn't worked out. In those situations, you have to say to yourself that you've learnt a lesson and that now you must move on. I've never looked back in my life. The minute you do that, you're finished.

4

BUILDING A TEAM

Pippa Dee

School Care was my crash course in business management, and although ultimately it had failed, the experience had provided me with a range of skills that I could put into practice in the following years. It had also provided me with a reputation, and no sooner had our demise been made public in that February of 1975, than the phone began to ring. I was contacted by all sorts of interested parties who wanted me to work for them.

Alan Richardson was a marketing man I'd known back in my days at Littlewoods. He'd now moved to a company called Pippa Dee, and he made the suggestion that I meet his MD, Ken Stephenson, who was also ex-Littlewoods, where he'd been buying controller on childrens' wear, and therefore my overall boss before I left. Ken was a very bright man, and I loved getting into long discussions with him about the different aspects of retailing: marketing, merchandising, pricing, ranging, the people in the business. . . . If I look back on my life as a retailer, I identify Ken as the person who influenced me most on producing a quality product, one of the crucial ingredients of Next's success. Ken had made all the policy decisions about children's wear at Littlewoods. His problem had been that the company lacked a coherent overall buying policy, with the result that we had terrific kids' clothes selling alongside ladies' wear of inferior quality. All the buyers did their own thing, and the resulting variety of product was one of Littlewoods' greatest weaknesses. Merchandise being sold under a store's name – whatever the department – should look as if it's been bought by one pair of eyes, and not by dozens. Ken Stephenson could see where Littlewoods was going wrong, and we used to discuss the problem at length, but he wasn't in a position to change the corporate approach.

At Next I was to learn from Ken's difficulties at Littlewoods, and our consistency of product was to be our greatest asset. Pippa Dee was an unusual company, whose main area of business was selling lingerie at parties – rather like Tupperware. They were part of a group called Rossgill Holdings Ltd, who had also set up other ventures, the main one being a chain of supermarkets called Moneysave. Pippa Dee's idea was that I should join them as a general manager of a new schoolwear subsidiary – in other words, I would be able to carry on with my School Care concept under a bigger, and presumably more permanent, umbrella. The offer appealed, but what really swung it for me was that Rossgill was short of good people, and was prepared to let me bring my senior team with me: the key people who had supported me through my troubles, and with whom I'd developed a very close relationship.

One of the reasons why I've been able to make a swift impact on any business I've moved into, is that I've always brought my team with me. The team I found at Pippa Dee included Colin Shiner, whom I'd worked for back in the Littlewoods days. And I complemented this with a senior merchandise controller, Chris Fagan (also from Littlewoods), a senior buyer, Bob Williams, warehouse manager, Arthur Ray, systems manager Charles Quinn, as well as sales personnel. Many of these people would be vital to our success at Next.

That March, we moved down to Burton-on-Trent, where Pippa Dee had its headquarters, and we spent the following weeks working night and day out of a pub called the Dog and Partridge. I was very excited by the project and anxious to get our part of the business up and running as quickly as possible.

I was enjoying the luxury of working on my own terms for a large public company that appeared to be doing so well. I was soon to discover, however, that appearances can be deceptive. One morning in March I walked into the head office to discover that two of the company's top people had been fired: one was Ken Stephenson, the Managing Director of Pippa Dee, and the other was Merchandising Director John Lloyd, a Pippa Dee founder and another former Littlewoods' employee.

Ken's leaving in particular shocked me. His departure alerted me to the fact that there was something badly wrong at Pippa Dee. You could argue that I was naïve not to check the business's financial ratings before joining the company. Today I would be able to read the signs and identify the problems, but at the time there was no reason for me to doubt that the business was doing well – they were a public company with large and impressive head offices, after all. Ken Stephenson's sacking, however, stirred up a hornets' nest, and I began to see that Pippa Dee's difficulties were rooted in a troubled past.

When the company had been set up eight years previously, its business was purely the sale of synthetic lingerie through the party plan method. Members of the 7,000-strong salesforce would organize parties in their area, take the goods along in suitcases and sell them to their friends and neighbours. In those days, as I say, synthetic fabrics, nylon, polyester, were highly acceptable. Pippa Dee's early success led to flotation. That's where the rot set in. It was a classic situation: the people who had driven the business received large lump sums on flotation – £50,000 to £100,000 in some cases. They lost the incentive to innovate and push the business forward just at the moment when it needed it more than ever before. Pippa Dee began to stagnate. John Lloyd, the Merchandise Director, failed to update the by now tired lingerie concept. Meanwhile, other Rossgill ventures were simply not taking off. From a flotation price of 80p, shares had dropped to 4p in 1975. The company results, announced four months after my arrival, showed a loss of £1 million.

This, then, was the situation into which I had brought my team so optimistically. We'd left one set of problems behind, only to find ourselves plunged into another crisis.

With the firing of Ken Stephenson and John Lloyd, two major jobs were now vacant. A man who'd worked as a consultant to the business, David Peel, was brought in as the new Managing Director, and I was asked to come on the Main Board as Product Director. Effectively this would mean that my priorities would now be the welfare of the group as a whole, and not merely that of my schoolwear division.

Within four weeks of my new appointment, I along with the rest of the Board was summoned to ICFC (Industrial and Commercial Finance Corporation) in London. During my years at Next, I would have many dealings with investment banks, and would become very familiar with the workings of the City, but this was my first experience of a City institution. ICFC was the merchant bank that had underwritten Pippa Dee's flotation, and because the float hadn't been successful, they'd been left with 29% of the stock. Barclays were the bankers to the business, and they put up most of the overdraft Pippa Dee required, but ICFC always had to top up that loan; if, for example, the bank were giving us an overdraft facility of £1 million, ICFC would provide a further £200,000. They were therefore bound to be concerned about Pippa Dee's increasingly poor performance. I'll never forget that first meeting with ICFC; I recall telling them about my plans for a coordinated range of ladies' clothing, to supplement the lingerie concept, and I spoke about the hopes I had for this new project. They gave us a lovely lunch, and afterwards one of the men from ICFC, a fellow from Bolton (I remember that, because I thought to myself, 'he's a Lancastrian, so he must be all right!'), stood up and said to us, 'Gentlemen, I'm very sorry to have to say that we're not prepared to support you any longer. We're not going to give you any more top-up finance'. He then turned to our Chairman, Jim Ingles, and continued: 'We've looked at the figures and we've discussed the situation, and we cannot give you any more than four weeks in which to turn the business round. We'll review the situation in a month, and if there's no change, I regret that you'll have to sell the business or face the consequences – you certainly can't continue to trade as things are.'

The Illusion of Choice

'Oh no, here we go again,' I thought. The onus was on my team and me, as Product Director, to produce the new range we'd promised and somehow to transform Pippa Dee's fortunes with its success. In four weeks. We certainly drank a few beers on the train back home to Burton-on-Trent.

It was June, and somehow we got through that first month without exceeding our overdraft limit. And the next. Then, with the launch of the new coordinated range that August, we began to pull the business back from the brink. We would close down the schoolwear concept, and concentrate our efforts on Pippa Dee ladies' wear and Dee Minor, the kids' wear range which was also sold by the party plan method. Sometimes you have to make that sort of choice in a business – it's better to do two things well, than three things badly. It was a question of people, and getting the right team for the job; I didn't want to dilute the team across the three parts of the business, and when it came to the toss-up, it was easier to run down the schoolwear concept than either of the other two. The average party value (i.e. the average takings at any one party) rose from £70 to £95, and the word came back from our salesforce that their customers liked the new range of ladies' wear in particular. Not only was it a quality product of exceptionally good value, but it was also a carefully edited range of merchandise, coordinated so that the customer could put together outfits with ease.

I had been refining my ideas on buying. In those days people's sense of fashion was less sophisticated than it is today, and any retailer who *helped* the customer by providing coordinated ranges, colour blocking and so forth, was, I believed, bound to be on to a winner. The trouble was, only the most exclusive names – like Jaegar and Mondi – were answering to this need. Most stores applied the 'system' I'd encountered at Littlewoods, where you'd have a skirt buyer and a blouse buyer who operated on different floors of the building and often didn't even meet, let alone consult one another on buying coherent ranges. This led not only to inconsistency of quality of product within the shop but also an incompatibility of styles. Women had to put up with shops where merchandise was displayed as in a bazaar. Even at Marks and Spencer the customer would be confronted with a bewildering choice of garments, none of which appeared to complement the others. The policy of buyers at the time was to purchase *everything* in the hope that *something* would sell. What this meant was that from the shop's point of view, there was enormous wastage, with vast areas of shop space devoted the year round to marked-down goods. Money was pouring out of retail businesses.

The peculiar nature of Pippa Dee's selling methods dictated a small range. Unlike the High Street, we had no choice but to edit mercilessly our selection of goods. Each of our saleswomen could carry only two suitcases-full of clothes to any one party, and our range was therefore bound to be limited by how much we could fit into the cases. Clearly we weren't going to be able to show fifty dresses, so we'd have to show seven of the best instead. There are some obvious advantages to this approach: if you have a small range, each of your lines is likely to sell at a higher rate than if you have a large range, and the offshoot is that you can buy the lines in bulk from your supplier – at a cheaper price.

Given the constraints of space, we decided to put together a range of clothes that could be purchased either singly or as part of a coordinated set – so, we would have a blouse that went with a skirt that went with the knitwear and so forth. Psychologically, the coordination worked on the customer: rather than buying individual garments, they always wanted to buy the other items that made up the outfit. It was an extraordinary discipline from our point of view, and the exercise taught me one of the keys to success in retailing: if you give the customer too much choice, you aren't going to make any money. The trick is to give the *illusion* of choice. In other words, rather than offering up thirty skirts, you give a selection of eight – the eight *right* skirts in a variety of colours. Next became synonymous with this method of merchandising, and spawned many, many imitators. But long before Next, we were doing it at Pippa Dee.

When I look back over the years, there is little doubt in my mind that Pippa Dee was the most demanding of the businesses I've worked for. The nature of the business imposed a whole series of disciplines that would stand me in good stead in the years to follow. At School Care I had learned the importance of getting the right supply structure, and at Pippa Dee this proved to be just as true – although perhaps for a different set of reasons. Principal among these was the way in which we paid our salesforce. They received no salary, but made their money on commission alone – 30% of all sales *irrespective of whether or not we were actually able to deliver the goods to the customer.* So, if a saleswoman took three orders for a £5 dress, she would automatically receive her £4.50 commission, even if we then failed to supply the dress. The system was a powerful incentive for us to get our supplying absolutely right.

The salesforce also kept us on our toes with regard to quality and price – again, because of the commission-only system. Naturally, if the clothes had been inferior or over-priced, there would have been few sales; without the sales we would have lost the salesforce; without the salesforce we would have no business. Why go through the hassle of arranging a Pippa Dee party if you aren't going to make any money?

These women were one of the most highly professional teams that I have worked with, largely because the commission system soon weeded out the weak performers. The rewards were there for those who wanted them, and were prepared to put in the hours; indeed the elite saleswomen actually earned more than the company directors – some of them were making up to £25,000 a year – and that was for part-time work. This feature of the business bred a natural democracy. Nobody respected me because I was Product Director; any respect I earned came because I produced good merchandise and good ranges. There was no sense of hierarchy; if you had no talent, these women had no time for you – even if you were the 'boss'. That's how it should be in business: too many employers believe that they own their staff, and can treat them as subordinates; while too many employees believe they have the right to be paid for doing nothing. Of course you can't always have everyone working on commission only, but the system implanted in me a belief in mutual respect between employer and employee. I still hold that belief.

People Management

Pippa Dee taught me so much about people management and staff motivation. When people work for themselves (as our salesforce did), they aren't scared to walk away if they are unhappy with the job. We knew we had some good people working for our salesforce, and that the business depended upon them. We knew that they could up and leave at any time, because they were self-starters and they had that confidence you gain when you work for yourself.

One of the most popular things the company did, and which inspired in the salesforce a tremendous team spirit, was the bi-annual sales conference. These terrific jamborees brought together women from all over the country, and combined training elements with having a good time.

The idea was an American one, and although it's fairly prevalent these days, no other retailer was doing it at the time I was with Pippa Dee. The women would arrive at the venue for a 9.30 start. It was a great day out, and all of them made a real effort to look good – even though many would have risen at 4 a.m. in order to be there on time. The conference would then fall into two parts, the first of which we called 'recognition', where we presented awards for outstanding achievement. We would start out by getting the different regions to identify themselves, which always provoked a lot of noise and good humour. Then we would call up on stage all the women who had achieved particular targets, and having handed them their bonus cheques, we would get them to join in some game or other on stage. There would be some fun, when they would compete to throw darts at a picture of the Chairman's face, or whatever, to win something like a canteen of silver. We would then call up everyone who had achieved their individual sales targets, and each of them would be given a bonus cheque. We'd have hundreds of them up there on the stage, all being recognized and thanked for their efforts, and all feeling part of the whole organization. They were wonderful moments. There would always be some sales message at this stage, and the training manager would come up and talk about selling skills and demonstrate various techniques – so there was a message too, but it was always with a party atmosphere. This was not your usual sales conference. One of the bonuses for me was using my three children – Melanie, Emma and Alex – to model the children's wear. On one unforgettable occasion, Alex, who was only three at the time, decided to have a 'rest' in the middle of the show, and sat herself down at the edge of the stage. She brought the house down!

The second part of the day was the fashion show, where we'd present the new range to the salesforce. That's where I had my input. It had been part of the conference before I'd joined Pippa Dee, but I brought an extra razzmatazz to the event. In the past they had used women from the office to model the clothes, but I brought in professional models and developed a style of my own on stage. (Actually, one of those same models, Denise Olive, was to work for me as a house model right through my time at Next.) I even brought in a choreographer to rehearse the show.

Those saleswomen really knew what they liked. If the range met with their approval, they'd be on their feet cheering, ringing bells and sounding klaxons. But if they didn't, there would be a terrible stony silence. Every conference was better than the one before, and each time we introduced improvements. One year we actually took the fashion show on the road for two weeks. We travelled around the country, presenting the show to the salesforce and then going back to the hotel to party afterwards. It was a great trip, and one in which the whole team built up tremendous camaraderie. The corporate culture we would develop at Next was rooted firmly in experiences such as these.

As we improved our product range, so I brought together and consolidated my team. I've already mentioned the importance of having a coherent buying policy, so that it *appears* that all your product has been selected by a single pair of eyes. And one of my strengths has been to bring together a team of people who are able to work together and achieve that common vision. At Pippa Dee I was really able to put this philosophy to the test. The team working under me all had their separate skills, but their goal was a shared one, and the resulting product range was a team effort.

From the outset one of the key team members was Thiry Thompson, who had actually started as a secretary and worked her way up into a buying job. She had a strong sense of style and a high level of taste, and she was largely responsible for the success of our early ranges. It was she who brought in, as a trainee buyer, a young woman who would come to have a profound impact on the rest of my life.

A Philosophy of Buying

Liz Devereaux-Batchelor joined Pippa Dee a couple of years after me. The first thing I noticed about her was her straightforward manner. She wasn't a great talker, but if you asked for her opinion, she would give it to you absolutely truthfully. This struck me early on when we hit problems with one of our manufacturers, a Midlands supplier of bras and corsets. We'd had a lot of complaints from customers about the quality of their garments, and several people had returned the goods to us. This, of course, was costing us money, as we still had to pay out the commission to our salesforce. I was puzzled, for this is the sort of problem you can expect with a fashion garment, but not with what we call the basics. We were debating the issue at a meeting, when I turned to Liz and asked her what she thought was wrong. She said quite simply, 'It's because the garments don't fit.' Many people in her position would have kept their mouths shut, for fear of causing offence, or to protect the person they were working for. Not Liz. Her attitude was that business was business and she wasn't interested in deceiving me to protect herself or anybody else. She then got up and outlined the problem, making drawings of the garments to show me precisely where the weaknesses lay. She was brilliant because she knew the product inside-out.

The incident made a lasting impression upon me. Hitherto, my buying philosophy had been geared towards price negotiation, but now here was someone showing me that there's little point in getting a good price out of a manufacturer if the manufacturer isn't going to make the garment well. I might think I've done a good job negotiating the price of a pair of jeans down from £5 to £4.80. But if the jeans are badly constructed and they don't fit, they're not even worth £4.80. Liz had a technical background – she had a first class degree at Leicester Polytechnic in Contour Design, which meant that she understood how garments were made – and her arrival at Pippa Dee changed my buying philosophy. When I came to set up Next, it was people with technical backgrounds – like Liz – whom I brought in as buyers.

We were pretty happy at Pippa Dee; we'd saved the situation, and things were now moving forward. Having got ladies' wear back on its feet, we were able to turn our attention to Dee Minor, the children's wear range. There were all sorts of other improvements we began to make in the business. On the merchandising side, I started buying from the Far East, thus increasing our profit margins, and I also introduced colour catalogues for the first time, which proved a marvellous success. In the past, the salesforce had been provided with large plastic folders containing photographs of the range. Because the range changed so frequently, this system had actually proved itself both expensive and inefficient – it relied on the salesforce inserting the new pictures whenever they arrived in the post. And more often than not, they failed to do this. I decided it would be better to have a single catalogue every six months, containing the total statement for that season. We also developed a small card which contained all the details of the garment in question – its price, the colours and the sizes it came in, etc. On the other side of the card we would attach swatches of fabric showing the different colourways. This meant that the salesgirl needed only to take one sample of the garment to a party; customers who wanted to order other colours and sizes had all the information they needed on the card, which was attached to the sample garment. Hitherto we had simply provided loose swatches of fabric, which invariably were lost. Our new approach was not only more professional, it was also foolproof, and it boosted sales immediately. Often it is the small things like that that are entrepreneurial, and which make a business work – you have to accept that people are fallible (and our salesforce was no exception), that loose swatches of fabric get lost and loose photographs don't get put in brochures. You've got to try and overcome those problems and that's what practical marketing is all about. A third thing we did was produce a broadsheet twice a year, containing all our sale stock. It worked brilliantly. Such ideas sound obvious, but most of the best marketing ideas are: it's when you start trying to be too clever that you go off the rails.

By 1979 we had turned the situation round and were back in profit. However, in spite of what was now a very healthy business situation, following an impressive turnaround, our share price was still pretty low, principally because the City simply didn't understand our peculiar way of selling. We'd climbed from a market price of 4p to 28p, but this still meant that we were highly undervalued on the stock market.

The Fight for Pippa Dee

Nevertheless, I knew that the company, in a remarkably short period of time, had achieved something of a business miracle. I was surprised, therefore, to receive a phone call from the Chairman, Jim Ingles, one day late in 1979, telling me that David Peel (the Managing Director) would be 'leaving us' shortly. I had always got on well enough with Jim Ingles, but I remember he was on £40,000 a year but that although he'd pop in from time to time to see how we were getting on, he had very little involvement in the day to day business. His call about David Peel's imminent 'departure' immediately struck me as odd, as David was away on holiday in America at the time. David may not have been a whizz-kid, but he was a very nice man, and someone I respected. He was both my boss and a friend, and I was surprised – even shocked – by the news: *why hadn't David mentioned any of this to me before going away?*

Jim Ingles gave me the impression that David wanted to leave Pippa Dee, and then hurried on to tell me that his replacement was 'the most superb man I have ever come across'. When I asked him for a name, he refused, saying only that the man in question had recently been working for a family-owned business in Yorkshire. I suppose I was hurt that I'd been passed over. If anybody had saved Jim Ingles's business from bankruptcy, it was the merchandising department, and I felt that I should have been considered for the now-vacant position of MD. Jim Ingles then launched into glowing praise of my work at Pippa Dee; he claimed that I had a great future with the company, that the new man's arrival would bring expansion and the possible managing directorship of a Pippa Dee subsidiary. It was cold comfort to me.

I will rarely take no for an answer, and if information is deliberately withheld from me, I will do my best to discover that information for myself. That evening I left the office an unhappy man, and when I got home I immediately phoned my old friend John Fishbourne. John did business with a whole host of companies in the North of England, and I knew that if anyone was going to help me trace this mysterious prospective MD, it would be him. He came right out with the answer: 'George, it can only be one guy. His name is Mark Dixon and he's just left Colliers (part of the United Drapery Stores group). He's been in and out of three jobs in as many years, but he's a great spieler, so he always comes across brilliantly in an interview.'

I had my answer, and the next day I went to see Jim Ingles. 'The guy you're hiring,' I told him, 'is called Mark Dixon. He doesn't have a very good track record, and I think you're making a mistake.' Jim Ingles was quite taken aback by my revelation. 'How on earth do you know this?' he asked me. 'I'm paid to know that sort of thing, Jim,' I replied. I then added that I didn't believe Ingles had the authority to appoint Mark Dixon without the Board's approval. An opinion with which he chose to disagree.

I had put my marker down. Now that I knew who was about to be foisted upon us, it was no longer just a question of my wounded pride. Pippa Dee was an unusual business, and the company needed someone at the head of it who understood it. If the new man had been of the right calibre, I might have accepted him, but I knew that Mark Dixon would not be suited to the business we'd all worked so hard to rebuild, and I wasn't going to take his appointment lying down.

I spoke to David as soon as he returned from America. It emerged that he had never really wanted to give up his Managing Directorship, but that he had been demoralized by Jim Ingles. I told him we had to fight Ingles's decision, and he immediately agreed. Ron Kite, the Finance Director, took the same view and we also engaged the support of Brian Hale, the Sales Director, and a non-executive Director called Little of Long Eaton Fabrics, one of our suppliers. At the following Board Meeting, when the matter of Mark Dixon arose, Jim Ingles was outvoted by 5-2, and shortly afterwards we ousted him as Chairman.

It was a tremendous blow to him, and thereafter the Mark Dixon issue became part and parcel of Jim Ingles's crusade to get back the company he looked upon as his own. He had something like a 20% share in Pippa Dee, and he now approached ICFC, to see if they would sell him their 29% stake. With 49% of the shares he would only need a few more to gain control of the company. The Board too went to ICFC who declared that they would support management – us, in other words. We could see the battle wasn't over by any means, and we re-inforced our ranks, bringing in County Bank as our financial advisers, and an old lawyer friend of mine: John Roberts. Other rumours of Jim Ingles's activities began to reach our ears: we heard that he was trying to get a variety of people to buy the business so that he could return as Chairman and put Mark Dixon in the MD's seat. A Yorkshire company called Stroud Riley Drummond was asked to put in a bid for us, but nothing came of it.

A small London-based retailing and manufacturing company called Amber Day approached us and said they'd very much like to take over the business. Given that we were making profits approaching £1 million that year, and yet were still only valued at £2½ million, it was easy to see why they saw us as a 'good buy'. They said, however, that they would only move in if they had the unanimous backing of the Pippa Dee Board. We wrote back politely, thanking them for their interest, but saying that we were fine as we were, and would rather retain our independence.

Three months later, Amber Day had decided they no longer required the backing of Pippa Dee management. They wrote to us saying that they had signed irrevocable agreements with Jim Ingles and ICFC, which meant that should they – Amber Day – bid for the business, the whole 49% would become theirs. Jim Ingles had imposed one condition upon them: *that were the deal to come off, Mark Dixon should become the Managing Director of Pippa Dee.*

We called in our advisers, John Roberts the lawyer and David Cardale from County Bank. David asked us if we four – Brian Hale, Ron Kite, David Peel and myself – would be prepared to resign in the event of a bid from Amber Day. We immediately said that we would be, well aware of the fact that the likelihood of actually having to do so was pretty high. But principles are principles and I wasn't prepared to be bought out; I knew that Amber Day would be wrong for the business, and if you really want to win any battle, you have to be prepared to fight to the very last. I have always stood up against things I haven't believed in, and sometimes at a great personal cost – you have to if you aren't going to compromise your integrity. A nasty period followed during which we put up a spirited defence. I remember being contacted by the Chairman of Amber Day, Ronnie Metzke, who told me that he recognized my role in transforming the company's fortunes, and who tried to coax me over to his side with offers of a bigger salary and a better car. I wasn't for sale and I wasn't interested.

In the end, the bid came through and Amber Day got their 51% stake and control of Pippa Dee. The day they went unconditional – a

Monday – I was asked, along with all the other Directors, to go to Jim Ingles's office in Lichfield. He was there with Mark Dixon and Ronnie Metzke. I was the first in, and they started off by telling me that they knew I'd been through a very difficult time, that I'd fought hard for a different result, but that they thought I was a great chap nonetheless, and they'd like me to stay on the Board – under Mark Dixon. Did they have my commitment? I replied that yes they did . . . but only twenty four hours at a time. 'While I'm working here,' I continued, 'I will work hard. But I cannot give any guarantee for the future, because I don't like to work for people who in my opinion have gone back on their word.' They didn't appreciate that very much – but I've never been afraid to voice my convictions.

The following Friday we were due to have a Board meeting. At 11.30 a.m. I received a note summoning me to one of the Boardrooms upstairs. There I found a man called Rose, from Amber Day's solicitors. He handed me an envelope, informing me that because I had said I could only give myself to the business on a daily basis Amber Day believed me to be in breach of contract, and that they therefore weren't obliged to pay me out. I then had to walk into the Board Meeting and sit through the business for the day, which was largely concerned with the takeover. I remember returning downstairs to my department, where all my staff were crying. It had been a terrible and cowardly way to dismiss me, and we were all very upset. I believe that if things don't work out in business, and you have to quit a company, you can do so with honour on both sides. Some years later, as a result of restructuring at Next, my Finance Director decided to leave. Gerry McLeod is still one of my closest friends today. I suggested to him that we should split his combined role of finance and systems, and that he would be most suited to running the systems/operations side. He went away, thought about my proposition, and returned to say that he was in agreement with me on the first count, but that he did not want to run systems/operations. He handled a difficult situation like a man, and fortunately we have remained great pals. He is a man with the highest integrity, and has been a great support to me personally. His departure from Next was a great loss, and a decision I have always bitterly regretted.

Eventually Amber Day did pay me out, but not before five months had passed. Within twelve months Mark Dixon was fired, and six months later Amber Day sold Pippa Dee back to the management. The principles I had stood by were vindicated.

Of course it was good to see my beliefs confirmed so conclusively, but in a way it didn't really matter to me any longer, for by that time I was deeply involved in creating a new business.

5

THE BIRTH OF NEXT

Hepworths

What nobody at Pippa Dee knew was that I had an ace up my sleeve. The day before my firing I'd had a meeting in Leeds with Hepworths – the men's wear group. It was County Bank who had put them in touch with me: I think they were impressed by the way in which I had stood up for what I believed in in the Amber Day affair, and they knew that Hepworths were looking for somebody to take on the planned launch of a new ladies' wear range. Thursday's meeting had been merely exploratory because I didn't seriously think I would be free to get involved. Friday I was fired. I telephoned Trevor Morgan, Hepworths' Development Director, straight away to say that I was free to have further talks about the project – so long as I could bring my team with me.

That Sunday Liz Devereaux-Batchelor, Bob Williams, Chris Fagan and a fellow called Ewart Mountford who was my Quality Control Director at Pippa Dee came with me to Ashby de la Zouche, where we lunched with Trevor Morgan. This was followed several days later by a meeting with the senior men at Hepworths: Jeff Rowlay, the Managing

44

Director, Ken Ashcroft, the Financial Director and Gerry McLeod who would become Financial Director when Ken was appointed Assistant MD that coming October. They told me more about their plans to develop in women's fashion which hung upon the purchase of a chain of high street stores codenamed 'K'. I later discovered that 'K' was actually Kendalls, an old Leicester-based family business, which had carved out a niche for itself in rainwear and which was known by the slogan 'Kendalls keeps you dry'. Sales had been hit by the exceptionally dry summer of 1976, and the company was now up for sale.

I went away, and together with Liz Devereaux-Batchelor and Bob Williams, put together some colour boards which showed our early ideas for a new ladies' wear concept. These we presented to the Main Board, which included Terence Conran, a non-executive Director who was shortly to become Chairman. I knew from my days with Pippa Dee that there was a wide gap in the market: at the bottom end there were scores of cheap and unstylish outlets, while at the top there were stylish goods at prices few people could afford. The customer I was aiming at was currently being forced into the bottom end of the market through lack of choice. I described her to the Hepworths board as someone whose taste level lay somewhere between Jaegar and Marks. At this stage it was just a hunch, but it was one that my subsequent research was able to bear up.

They must have liked our work, because shortly after that they invited me on board as a consultant. The deal they proposed was that during the next six weeks I should research the market and produce a report, outlining the ladies' wear concept. Should the purchase of 'K' go through, I would be engaged as Merchandise Director of the new business on a salary of £30,000. Should it fail, I would receive a compensation fee of £1,000, in addition to my salary for the six-week period. I was happy with the arrangement. Years later I was to learn that I could have negotiated better terms. When Next was buying Combined English stores in the summer of 1987, I was to discover just how much Hepworths had valued me. As I was leaving a meeting I bumped into Tony Haygarth, Finance Director at CES. 'I'm glad to meet you after all these years,' he said. When I asked him why, he continued, 'When we sold Kendalls to Hepworths, there was a clause in the contract stating that they would not go through with the purchase unless they could sign you on to run the new business.' Given that the Board at Hepworths rated me so highly, it does seem peculiar that they would be prepared to drop me in the event of failure to buy Kendalls. I believe that if you find someone good in business, you should hold on to them. The episode says something about the mentality of the Hepworth management, and although I could not interpret it at the time, was an ill omen for the future.

I signed my contract at the end of March 1981, and started work on the new concept immediately. I believed more than ever that there was a huge market for coordinated merchandise. I'd proved the principle at Pippa Dee already – in the early days even I'd been surprised at the rate at which people were buying our goods through this peculiar party plan method. I'd asked the salesgirls why, and they told me that it was because you could never get anything in the shops. If people bought that way through the party plan, then how much more would they buy on the High Street? Like my hunch about my prospective customer, it was only a strong feeling, and to confirm it I started to travel round the country visiting stores and seeing for myself if my instincts were correct.

My Brand of Market Research

I've been labelled in the past as someone who has little faith in market research, and with reason. Fashion is an inexact science, I don't believe that facts and figures can tell you nearly as much as going out into the High Street and seeing for yourself what is selling and what isn't. The best ideas don't start in an office, they start with the consumer. So I started researching the market in my own way; in other words, I spent some time analysing information we'd received from Kendalls and, more importantly, I visited fifteen of the key towns in which Kendalls had their stores – Birmingham, Hereford, Coventry, Cheltenham, Liverpool and Wolverhampton were among them. You can pick up a certain amount by standing in a shop and watching what is and what isn't selling, but what I found most useful was going out into the town and just talking to people on the street, in the supermarkets or whenever. I'd ask them where the best place for clothes was in their town, and more often than not the response would be, 'Oh, there's nothing much.' I remember Loughborough in particular, where I was told that the only decent shop was far too expensive and that the women always returned to Marks and Spencers in the end, because there was no affordable alternative. Once you've heard that story a few times, you begin to form the sort of comprehensive picture that no market researcher with a clipboard could ever concoct.

As I travelled round the country, so I looked at the competition, from the very top end of the market to the very bottom. Of the branded ranges on sale in department stores, it was Mondi, the upmarket German brand, that most impressed me with its stylish, high quality and colour coordinated range. But Mondi clothes were expensive, as were those of Jaegar, Reldan and Options. Country Casuals was slightly less expensive, and they had also achieved a coordinated look. However, the style was too 'county' for my liking, and the prices still put the clothes beyond the reach of the vast majority of shoppers. At the other end of the market – Etam, Top Shop, Chelsea Girl, Wallis – I found the 'buy-it-all' approach to stock that I've described before: the stores stocked as many styles as was possible, in the hope that something would sell. Inevitably, 25% of stock was always at reduced prices. Price levels varied, but were generally low, and quality was at best indifferent. The merchandise was aimed at the 16-25 age group, who had emerged as the big spenders in the 1970s. But now that these women had grown up, where could they buy their clothes? Marks and Spencers, inevitably, I investigated a number of their stores during the course of my research, and found some good quality garments at reasonable prices. There was, however, no coordination and most of the merchandise was pretty unstylish and basic.

All of this began to give me a strong impression of my market, and it was confirming the feeling that I'd had when I'd made my initial presentation to the Board at Hepworths. At times like this your mind works rather like a sponge, taking in everything, the large, the small, the upmarket and the downmarket. Eventually a vision emerges of what is right and what isn't. The vision that emerged for me was of a retail chain aimed at the 25-plus age group in the B, C1 and C2 market, which embodied style, quality, price and service.

Image-making

One of the things that had struck me was the lack of image among the retailers I'd visited. I would visit ten stores in an afternoon, and when I'd finished I'd have real trouble distinguishing one from another in my memory – all of them were quite lacking in any identity. This, I might add, was as true at Hepworths as anywhere else – I used to say that customers walked into a Hepworths store not because they'd seen the place and recognized it, but because they had turned left down the street instead of right! The one store that proved the exception to this dreary rule was Benetton. Back in those days few people in Britain had heard of them, as there were only the two stores, one in Knightsbridge and one in South Molton Street. Benetton was breaking many of the hallowed 'rules' of retailing, and the result was a fresh and appealing image. Unlike everyone else, they weren't using window dummies to display the merchandise – they simply draped items over black plastic fittings. When you got inside, the garments were displayed around the perimeter of the store, and rather than using the standard racks, the clothes were folded and piled high on shelves. There were strong colour statements and because the shop was small, it was easy for the customer to relate the skirts to the jumpers etc, and thus coordinate their own outfits. Like Pippa Dee, the range was narrow, and like Pippa Dee, the formula worked. There were queues outside those Benetton stores every day. I was impressed. Benetton reaffirmed my view that the most important thing you can do as a retailer is create a strong identity on the High Street, so that the public retains an image of the shop and recognizes it immediately they see it. Today, I'd say that the chain that has best achieved this is Anita Roddick's Bodyshop.

Kendalls, like practically everyone else in those days, had no image whatsoever. The stores were crammed with merchandise and there was no apparent range plan. The more I saw, the more I was convinced that I was going to have to start a new ladies' wear chain from scratch. The purchase of Kendalls would provide us with some excellent sites, but that was it. The shops would have to be gutted, redesigned and re-merchandised. We needed a new image and we needed a new name. I've always preferred starting with a blank sheet of paper; I think it's when I *haven't* started from scratch that things have gone wrong. Of course it always appears easier to have a leg-up in business, and it usually seems cheaper, but if you have a strong idea of what you want, then there's no alternative to going through the hard work of starting right from the beginning. I was to learn the truth of this lesson to my cost during the latter years at Next.

In May 1981 I was in Frankfurt attending the *Interstoff* fabric show, when the news came through that Hepworths had succeeded in buying Kendalls. I'd received a message to call Trevor Morgan, and I remember getting back to him from a call-box. It was by necessity a brief talk, because I only had a few marks, but there was enough time for Trevor Morgan to say that he had discovered that Kendalls had many more buyers than he had originally thought, and would it therefore be necessary for me to bring all of my team? What he meant was that he didn't think we needed Liz. I knew that we couldn't develop the concept without her. 'You've offered me £20,000,' I told Trevor, 'and Liz was supposed to be coming in on £7,000. If you can't afford that, take it out of my salary.' In short, I was telling him that I was only going to come if my whole team could come with me. Kendalls may have had an army of buyers, but it's talent that makes the difference between failure and success, and I knew that I couldn't succeed without Liz.

The following Monday we moved into Kendalls in St James Street, Leicester, ready to take over the reins of the business. It was a rickety old building, which should have been condemned years earlier. Trevor had been appointed Managing Director. He chose his office upstairs and set about dealing with the inevitable personnel problems that arise out of any takeover. Suddenly I felt at a loss. I was the man who'd been brought in with the concept and, although I was officially Assistant MD/Merchandise Director, there didn't seem to be any office for me. I decided that I would wander up to the buying floor. At least I would feel at home there. It was an open-plan arrangement, which I liked, and I soon found myself chatting away to the staff. One of them, a girl called Sue Johnson, pointed out the former Merchandise Director's office, and suggested I make it my own. No one could ever accuse that office of having pretensions! I remember looking across the buying floor (which was on at least three different levels, and covered with an unappealing selection of four carpets), and seeing this corrugated glass office. One of the panels had been knocked out, and replaced by a plain piece of glass. Through the doorway – the door was no longer there – I could see a table with a peeling formica top, and an assortment of metal canteen chairs with canvas seats. Still it was better than nothing, and solved my immediate difficulty.

But how was I to set about working? On the one hand, I was now in charge of a chain of stores that was still in business; on the other hand I had my new concept and I was eager to get on with it. How easy it would have been to simply ignore Kendalls, and concentrate on my project, but unfortunately that wasn't possible. For the coming months I would juggle the two jobs until we were able to phase out Kendalls by slashing prices at the January sales. As we reduced the stock, so we cleared more shops in preparation for what would become the new chain of ladies' wear stores – Next.

My team joined me there three weeks after I moved into Kendalls, having stayed on at Pippa Dee until the purchase had gone through. Sadly we were one short: Liz Devereaux-Batchelor, Bob Williams and Chris Fagan duly arrived, but Ewart Mountford decided at the last minute that he wouldn't come. He was my expert on quality and I was sorry to lose him, but there was nothing I could do about it.

We began to develop our concept, bringing to fruition the recommendations I had put forward following my weeks of research on the High Street. We had decided that the launch date of the new concept was February 1982, so we had a bare nine months in which to develop and produce what would become Next. Starting a new business can create the most wonderful team spirit, and I remember the period as one of the happiest times in my life. Of course there was a large measure of self-doubt, and occasionally I would stop and think to myself, 'This is crazy. Why should I do any better than anybody else on the High Street? What right have I to think I'm any different?' As a boy I used to look at the big chains of stores – Littlewoods and Marks and Spencer – and wonder how anybody could have built such large businesses. Some of that feeling returned during those months leading up to the launch of Next. But by far the strongest feeling was one of excitement and of knowing that we were doing something new that was going to be big.

Image was uppermost in my mind at the outset, and I knew that that image must start with the shop fitments. Back in April I had realized that I knew nobody who could design the shops for us. The Financial Director, Ken Ashcroft, suggested during one of our early meetings that I contact John Stephenson, who was the Design Director for Conran Associates. Terence Conran was, of course, on the Hepworth Board, and Conran Design had worked on Hepworth stores in Bath and Bristol, which were never highly successful, but which looked very smart. John and I met for the first time in Birmingham on 27 April, and it soon became apparent that we would work well together. I remember we spent the whole day visiting towns in the area, like Tamworth and Sutton Coldfield. We then visited Birmingham in depth, ending the day with a very late lunch at 4 p.m., during which we discussed everything we'd seen, and began to develop an idea for the look of the new chain of stores. John agreed with me that Benetton had achieved a strong image. The other shop which impressed us was Country Casuals where they had also moved the merchandise away from centre-floor, displaying it instead in pigeon-holes around the perimeter of the store. The clothes were, as I've said, pricey and too 'county' for my liking, but there was a definite sense of identity and an order which was lacking elsewhere in the High Street.

The store concept we developed with Conran Designs was to prove unique in many ways, and we slaughtered many a sacred cow. There would be no window dummies, and no racks of merchandise displayed in the middle of the store. There was a further, highly significant feature to our plan: usually when you redesign a store, you have to put up with teams of shopfitters who first gut the place and then rebuild it on site – the process can easily take eight weeks, and you either lose that period of business, or carry on with the builders around you. We wanted to be able to close each Kendalls shop, gut it and redesign it completely in a matter of *five days* – this would then enable us to have as many as fifty shops up and running within six weeks of our launch. So, we had the standard units built off site. This would also afford us the impact of arriving on the High Street, almost overnight, with a brand new image. We did a test run of the scheme in Kendalls' Stevenage store, the autumn before our launch. Although takings didn't immediately shoot up (after all, the merchandise remained unchanged), the experiment did prove to us that our system worked.

Trevor Morgan, as Development Director, was as involved as I with these plans. Our opinions diverged on a great number of issues, but I think that was the reason we worked so well together. It would have been very easy to spend a fortune on the design of the shop, but Trevor negotiated a fee with Conran Design which must go down in their records as the cheapest job they have ever done! We paid them £18,000 for the concept, which would have been a reasonable fee for one shop, but was a steal when you think that we were going to roll out sixty-five.

But although Trevor's careful attitude to money was to prove a real asset in most instances, it also led to some conflict. I remember the occasion he came to me, only a week after we had moved into the Kendalls building, and said, 'I don't think we'll go with your concept for the stores after all – they seem to be doing a great job at Kendalls.' I was furious, and said that if we didn't do the job properly, I wasn't prepared to stay on. In the back of my mind, I knew that if we were forced to make compromises, I would have to leave. I didn't really want to be out of a job again, but I knew that my reputation and professional integrity were at stake, and that I wasn't going to do things by halves.

To be fair to Trevor, there was some jealousy among the people at Hepworths, who wanted to know why so much money was being spent on the new ladies' wear range, when their side of the business was in dire need of attention. I believe that Trevor kept them at bay, thus giving me the freedom to get on with the job. There is little doubt in my mind that he was under considerable pressure from the Board, who had spent little on most of the declining Hepworths chain. Trevor and I had to persuade people it would be a false economy to hang onto Kendalls' brown carpets when the Next colour scheme was going to be grey. Terence Conran's influence was also a significant force for good. Had he not been on the Board, I'm sure I would have lost many of the battles I was to have with Hepworths over the new concept and its image. He represents a standard of excellence in design.

N-E-X-T

One of our greatest battles at that early stage was over the name of the new chain. Some of the Hepworths' directors weren't keen on any change at all, and felt that we could happily stay with 'Kendalls'. After all, changing the name meant changing the shop signs, and that cost money. I wouldn't give in on this issue, because a new concept must be launched properly. Having persuaded them of the wisdom of change, I then began to receive suggestions from Directors, their wives and anyone else you care to mention. Hundreds of suggestions came through, most with some sort of pseudo-French or Italian flavour, and none of which appealed to me at all. We were getting quite worried when John Stephenson rang me with an idea he'd had while flying back from a business trip in Switzerland. 'Write down the following: N – E – X – T.' 'Yes, I've got that,' I said. 'Go on.' 'That's it,' John replied, 'NEXT'. I looked at the word in front of me, and realized that it was brilliant: it represented both the immediacy of fashion and the sense of the future. And it wasn't a feminine name, which meant that should we want to develop into men's wear we could do so under the same name. Furthermore, 'Next' had a certain retentive quality, largely because it's an adjective. Let me explain: if you say 'I'm going to Next,' people will think, 'Next what?' so it creates a question in the mind, which is good.

I went home that evening, having had a mixed response from my colleagues. As I walked through the door, I met Melanie, my eldest daughter, who must have been about 14 at the time. She asked me if I'd thought of a name, and when I said 'Next,' she laughed and said it was absurd. I was disappointed, and three hours later I said to Melanie, 'Do you really think the name's so bad?' 'Next?' she replied. 'Oh yes, I think it's awful.' Melanie's capacity to remember anything we ever spoke about was pretty limited then – she was only interested in boys. This was the first time she'd remembered anything I'd said for as long as three hours, and I thought, 'Well, that's it. If Melanie can retain NEXT after one brief conversation, then it's got to be the right name.'

Jeff Rowlay, the Managing Director at Hepworths, didn't share my enthusiasm for 'Next', and insisted we get some market researchers in to test it out on our potential customers. I have a vivid memory of a man from the company we used coming to see me in Leicester, and telling me that 'Next' had been roundly rejected by his sample groups. Evidently it had all the wrong connotations, and made people think of 'next-to-nothing' and – more strangely – 'ex,' as in ex-husband or wife. I wasn't going to leave it at that, and I immediately went down to London to see John Stephenson and another of the Conran designers, Tina Ellis. I knew that they, like me, thought the name was brilliant, and my proposal was that we should carry out our own bit of market research. What we did was to design a range of carrier bags for a variety of different stores. Among these was a beautiful grey bag with a burgundy handle and the logo 'next' printed in lower case letters. They were given to Marplan whose brief it was to ask people what sort of shop they thought each bag represented. Marplan gave a presentation of their findings to the Hepworth board in Leeds. The girl started with the Benetton bag, which apparently had had little success. Nobody outside London had heard of Benetton in those days, and the response had been very negative. 'But you should see the queues in Knightsbridge,' I couldn't help thinking. When they got to 'Next,' the response was quite different. The overwhelming reaction was that this was a shop that would probably sell ladies' coordinates, that people would aspire to it, but that it would probably be too expensive for your average shopper. That was precisely the image we sought, so 'Next' it was going to be.

Many years later, I was to discover how John had *really* come up with 'Next'. I was staying at the home of a great friend of mine, Roger Seelig, when a phone call from John came through, inviting Roger for lunch that day. I hadn't seen John for four years, and he invited me along too: by an extraordinary coincidence, the day happened to be 12 February 1989 – the anniversary of the launch of Next! John confessed that he had originally thought of the name when he was working at Burton in the early seventies. They had planned a young leisurewear range which never actually happened. The name, along with the concept, had been shelved. John had always liked it, but he was wise enough to realize that I wouldn't take to it knowing it was a Burton reject. He was absolutely right, and I'm grateful to him for not telling me.

There's one more anecdote about the name that's worth telling:

54

after the launch of Next, demand was so high we began having trouble maintaining our stock levels. A woman wrote to me saying that 'Next week' might have been more appropriate a name than 'Next'. I think it's the only time I ever doubted our decision!

Now we had the name, but with three months to go there was much work to be done. We needed to find the right suppliers, establish relationships with them, and set up the merchandising systems. We had inherited at Kendalls an attitude to buying which was, to be fair, the approach prevalent in most retailing organizations at the time but which wasn't one we shared. I remember one buyer had bought 10,000 striped dresses which were selling at the rate of about eight a week – we had several years' supply there which took no account of changing fashions! Then there was the consignment of garments from India, which had been packed during the monsoon, and which emerged from the boxes covered in dead flies.

New Product Development

At Pippa Dee I had learned the importance of quality control, and I applied those lessons at Next. We would control our product right the way through, from the raw materials to the finished garment in the shop. While in other organizations the majority of buyers were coming in half-way through the process, at Next we would be making the decisions about every dye batch and every button. It's attention to that sort of detail that gives you the quality of garment we had in mind. It meant a lot of work, and it also meant – as we had done at Pippa Dee – tracking down the manufacturers who understood our philosophy. There's no doubt that we were making life more difficult for ourselves, because it takes time to develop a business where your manufacturing and retailing arms are inter-related. It's much easier simply to let someone else get on with making the garments while you concentrate on selling them. But we knew the potential reward was great, that if you and your manufacturer share a master plan, you can move forward together and make a concerted attack on the market.

It's technically very difficult to sell coordinated separates, because different dye batches come out of the cloth mills in varying tones. And many people told us it would be impossible for us to achieve the quality in the bulk we required. Indeed it would have been if we'd bought like everyone else, who would simply go down to London each week and ask the suppliers, 'What have you got today, mate?' But the plan to sell coordinated separates made it doubly important to set up systems whereby we controlled every step, to go right back to the yarn that was used in each garment. Liz was a key player in the process, and she was highly demanding. Sometimes we would be wanting to finalize a garment and she'd be worrying about getting the right buttons – it's those touches which make the difference.

This process is called product development, and it was a fundamental aspect of our philosophy at Next. Quite apart from giving us a quality product, it allowed us to react to trends swiftly and repeat on the winning ranges. In short, it gave us a flexibility that nobody else on the High Street possessed, and it also kept our prices down. Where the normal procedure in other chains would be to buy your complete season of, say, shorts in a single batch, we would organize it so that we only bought perhaps eight or nine weeks' worth at a time. If you order *before* you see the trends developing (as most people do), the only way you are going to make money is by pushing up your prices, thus increasing your margins and offsetting the waste of unsold merchandise. We avoided that waste because we weren't buying everything in advance; as the season progressed, we were able to react to changing trends and give the customer exactly what she wanted. The wraparound top in a knitted fabric, known as a ballet wrap, was a major fashion influence in 1988, and is a good example of this process. Most of our buying decisions had to be made ten months before the season began, so in March 1987 we knew that the ballet top was going to emerge as one of the garments for Spring 1988. There was no way of telling how strong it was going to be, but three or four weeks into the season we could see that the garment was moving fast. Having the controls and the systems we could then order more, according to demand. We sold 92,000 that year, but there was also a positive knock-on effect on conventional knitwears and ladies' shirts. It's a highly complex operation, because it relies on maintaining your stock levels absolutely right. But that's what retailing is about, and that's the difference between a retailer and a shopkeeper, a retailer is someone who actually understands the consumer, and develops his product from the design and the yarn through to the marketing and sale of the finished garment, while a shopkeeper enters the process 80% down the line, and has no involvement with, or understanding of, the product.

The sophisticated buying system we developed was made possible only by the relationships we built with our suppliers, some of whom I'd known from as long ago as my Littlewoods days. As I've said, the strength of any retailer lies in his supply structure – the supply structure is the veins and arteries of any retail operation. It's only through having the right relationship with your supplier that you can react to trends in the way I've described; the minute you start seeing your sales patterns develop at the beginning of, say, the Spring season, your supplier has to start producing more merchandise according to those patterns, and to do so, he will have had to hold cloth in stock for you and keep production open for you into February. In the case of the ballet top, we were able not only to react to demand very swiftly, but even to bring in variations on the range in mid-season.

Not many people make the effort that's required to develop this sort of relationship with suppliers – and yet the potential rewards are as high. One business that did impress me some years later, was the small German chain of stores, Biba, which we acquired with the Combined English Stores purchase. They, like us, operated with a very tight team. They kept their stockholding low and were always right on top of their product.

The Right Price

I had always felt the tailored jacket was a garment that could really establish Next as the place where fantastic value and high quality walked hand in hand. In clothing there are certain key items, and the price you set for those items will establish the tone of the rest of your store. Because the tailored jacket is the hardest garment to make well, it's always quite dear. If we could bring the price of our jacket down, yet retain the quality, I knew that people would notice. I took the view, then, that it would pay to have a high quality garment made and that I would reduce my profit margins so that the jacket would be seen as excellent value. I knew nobody who made tailored jackets, so I contacted

Bob Russell, who was MD at Hepworth Retail, for advice. He put me on to a number of his suppliers, one of which was a major South African manufacturer called Rex Truform. They were actually the most expensive on the list, but they were also the best. I remember them sending us some samples. While most people would deliver samples in plastic bags, these garments arrived in a presentation box, which looked rather like a coffin. All the clothes were beautifully displayed, and it was hard to believe they had travelled such a distance. Later, when I went to South Africa to visit the factory, it was the same story: the place was pristine. I knew we had found a supplier who shared our high standards.

I think it's fair to say that in 1981 South Africa was not as sensitive an issue for the businessman as it is today. Through the years of our relationship with Rex Truform, I became increasingly aware of the prejudice and political injustice of the place – I especially remember being appalled when I learned that it was illegal for a black and a white to marry. Marriage to the person you love seems to me to be the most basic human right. Next actually had a disagreement with Rex Truform, and we therefore exited from our South African connection on business grounds. Even without those grounds, however, I believe we would have pulled out. I don't know the final answer to the sanctions debate, but I have come to believe that it is worth fighting for liberties, and that there is often a cost involved.

So our jacket was going to be a major plank in our marketing strategy. It would establish in the customer's mind that Next stood for both quality and value. We had to get it right. At Country Casuals, jackets were retailing at around £70, while at Jaeger people were paying between £90 and £100. If we could bring in a jacket at under £50, but of similar quality, we would be on to a winner. In the end, we brought the jacket out at £49.99, with the result that our profit margins were ten points lower than on any other item. We were entering the market, therefore, with a tailored jacket of exceptional value. The strange thing is, if you lower your margin, you very often end up making excellent profits, simply by virtue of the volume you achieve. It's better to sell five jackets and make a profit of £10 on each, than one with a profit of £25.

Customers are incredibly sensitive to price, and the relationship between price and value has always been fundamental to my retailing philosophy. As you move down the socio-economic scale, price, by necessity, is the most important factor. But in the ABC1 market, which is more discerning, many other criteria come into play, and value becomes as important as price; by value, I mean style, quality, presentation, service and all those other aesthetic qualities. If the price is a fair representation of all those elements, then the item is perceived to be of good value – and that's what we achieved with our jacket at Next. Of course you'll always have the odd person who will go to a 'designer' shop, buy a blouse for £500 and consider it good value because it's a one-off. But they're the exception.

I'll never forget the lesson I learnt from a Littlewoods buyer, Jack Butler, who was running a negotiation skills course I attended. He told me that *cost has nothing to do with price*. I might have a wonderful piece of pottery which cost me £40 from my supplier. Now, because I need to run my shop, I may decide to sell the pot for £80. The customer may, however, decide that £25 is all the piece is worth, and therefore doesn't buy it. The point is that when you're setting a price, you have to start with the customer, and not with whatever it has cost you to produce the goods. You need to know your market. You also need to have the right suppliers so that you can maintain your costs at a reasonable level. If you can increase the volume of sales per line, then, of course, you'll end up making more money. That's were we started at Next: good quality, good value, but not too high on exclusivity.

We worked on developing our range, bearing all these factors in mind. There was plenty of discussion between the members of the team, but it was all constructive because the team spirit was so strong. As buyers, Liz and Bob were naturally inclined to buy more stock, while Chris – the stock-controller – wanted to go the other way. I tried to keep a balance. We decided early on that we would base our range on four colours. This would not only create the coordinated look, but it would also give the impression of a wide choice. In fact the choice *was* there but in an edited form. Rather than having multiple ranges, we preferred to select the best lines and then produce each of these in the four colours. The look would be fashionable and stylish, and the prices accessible.

The London Fashion Scene

We'd decided that we needed a major PR launch – after all you can have the best product in the world, but it's not going to sell if nobody knows about it. We'd discussed the possibility of advertising, but felt it was both prohibitively expensive, and inappropriate to fashion. If you bombard the public with your name, in the way advertisers do with soups and soap powders, the name loses its exclusivity. We had always known that although we wanted to achieve volume, we also wanted to retain an impression of a measure of exclusivity. John Stephenson introduced me to a woman called Phyllis Walters, who ran her own PR agency in London, and who was to prove a powerful influence in the months leading up to the launch.

Phyllis was very much the London fashion PR lady, and I remember her initial visit to our dilapidated offices. When she arrived, her first question was how many designers did we have. We had none in the sense that she meant. But we did have two buyers in whom I believed: Liz, who had trained in contour fashion, and Bob, who was an expert in knitwear. I did wonder at that stage if, perhaps, I should adopt the more conventional approach, and employ a design studio. But in the end I didn't, and I never had cause for regret. Phyllis looked at some of our early sample merchandise and declared that with some work, she thought our concept would take off. She was a very forthright woman and throughout her involvement with Next, she would criticize us, and urge us to change the merchandise. Sometimes this hurt – and I think Liz and Bob, who were working so hard on getting the merchandise right, must have found Phyllis difficult to cope with. But we all listened to her, and took what she said on board. I believe that in the long run, her prodding did us good, for it kept us on our toes.

I knew nothing about London in those days, and deep down I was terrified of the London fashion scene. During the course of that Autumn of 1981, Phyllis introduced me to this new world, and I got to know many of the star writers: Sally Brampton who was then at the *Observer*, Brenda Polan at the *Guardian*, Gail Rolfe of the *Daily Mail* and Kathryn Samuels of the *Daily Telegraph*. Many of these people would become close friends over the years. It was Phyllis who decided that the best PR vehicle for our launch would be an eight-page advertorial promotion in *Vogue*, which is read not only by the consumer but also by the trade. She took me to meet Suzy Banks, who was in charge of special projects and Mandy Clapperton, the fashion promotions editor. We had a pleasant talk, but I'm sure their feeling was that here was a complete unknown – from the provinces – and that this new concept called 'Next' wasn't ever going to come to very much. I wasn't to be discouraged, however, and I invited them to Leicester with their photographer, John Bishop, to see some of our merchandise.

It wasn't just the merchandise I wanted them to see. It was the shop too. Trevor Morgan had originally conceived the idea of erecting a mock shop in a warehouse adjacent to our offices, principally as a means of testing out the modular units before we went live. The day the people from *Vogue* came to see us, the mock shop proved itself the most powerful weapon in our marketing armoury. I've mentioned my grim-looking office before, and I'm sure the *Vogue* team must have wondered if they were wasting their time as they sat on my assortment of canteen chairs, around the peeling formica table. Presently, I suggested we take a look at some of the clothes. I led them across the multi-level and multi-coloured buying floor, down a flight of stairs, through a warehouse and across the road to another ageing building. They followed me through a tiny door and up some back stairs which took us past racks of nasty Kendalls merchandise. At last, we reached a large blue sliding door, bolted and padlocked. I unlocked it and drew it back, switching on the lights. There before our eyes, in the most unpromising of settings, was a complete Next shop, designed and merchandised in the manner that would guarantee our success on the High Street a few months later. My guests' reaction was marvellous. They pounced on the mock shop and eagerly examined the clothes. The Next concept was there before their eyes, and I like to think they could see then that it would work. Next was never going to be about the fabulous, one-off designer garment, which is largely the stuff of fashion editors' copy. It was about practical, wearable, stylish and affordable clothes. And even fashion editors have mothers, sisters and friends. . . .

When it appeared the following February, our eight-page *Vogue* promotion elicited a response that even we had not expected. *Vogue* told me that their switchboard was jammed by callers wanting to know when their local Next store would open. Suzy Banks subsequently told me that Next still holds the record for response to a promotion.

It was Phyllis's idea to use the *Vogue* photographs with a press release we would send out to provincial newspapers. At the time, it was very unusual for PROs trying to reach a nationwide consumer to expend time and money on the provincial press. But Phyllis suggested this route largely because our London presence in the early stages of the launch was to be limited to a small shop in Victoria Street. The campaign she devised was planned months in advance, so that we could ensure copy on the day each of our shops opened. I think it's true to say that nobody had ever treated provincial journalists in the way we did. I spent time meeting them and taking them out, and we took them to see the mock shop. On a national level we organized it so that a variety of selected newspapers would come out with our story on different days. The major exclusives included Sally Brampton's terrific write-up in the *Observer*, the Sunday before our launch, and that was followed on the Monday by a piece in the *Daily Mail* by Gail Rolfe. These two features set the ball rolling: the appetite for Next stories had been created and our publicity just snowballed.

Nothing will ever beat the excitement of the weeks preceding our launch, as we busied ourselves with clearing the old Kendalls stock, planning the process of changeover for each store and training our sales staff. I strongly felt that I didn't want the gum-chewing sales assistants that were the norm on the High Street. The staff at Next would bring back the idea of service. There were inevitable hitches during those final weeks, principally on the stock side. We had one highly unnerving drama with a Czechoslovakian supplier who failed to deliver a jacket on time, and having planned to have all our stock in the warehouses by Christmas, we only had 50% in at the end of the year. They were very testing times, but not once did I ever consider putting back our launch date.

In mid-January, six weeks before the launch, we gave a fashion show at the Leicester Holiday Inn, to which all our Managers and Group Directors came. The form of the event harked back to my Pippa Dee days. Our Managers all thought the range fabulous. Then I remember Terence Conran, whom I'd only met on a couple of previous occasions, coming over to me at the end of the event and congratulating me warmly.

But of all the words of encouragement I received at that stage, those I remember with the most gratitude were spoken by Eric Crabtree, who was Deputy Chairman of Debenhams, a long-serving member of the Hepworths Board, and a man of great charm and style. 'George, my boy,' he said, 'if your concept doesn't work, it's not because you and your team have made any mistakes. It's because the great British public do not appreciate quality and style.' At a time when I was assailed by doubts, Eric's words were a tremendous boost to my confidence.

The Launch

When we did launch our first seven shops, on 12 February 1982, our takings on day one were 2½ times the amount we had estimated. And six weeks later we were having to put back the opening of some other shops, simply because the demand for Next clothes had depleted our stock supplies. Not even we had counted on the Next euphoria that would sweep the country. There are two incidents which I remember vividly, which sum up the impact Next was to have. As I was opening the store at Horsham, I started chatting to some of the customers, finding out what they thought of Next, and why they had come to shop there. One of the women told me that she had come all the way from Essex, as this was her nearest branch. I was amazed, but soon learned that other women were doing the same all over the country. The second thing happened on a train as I was travelling home to Leicester. I was sitting opposite an attractive and well-dressed young woman who was reading the *Vogue* in which Next featured. She was flicking through the magazine in a distracted fashion, but when she came upon our promotion she stopped short. She went through the eight pages very slowly, and when she'd finished, she turned to her boyfriend and said, 'Have you seen this?' I wanted to stand up and tell her that the promotion was mine, but I couldn't bring myself to do so. I knew, however, that we had taken off.

6

THE STYLE REVOLUTION

The Affordable Collectables

These were only the first signs of an apparently insatiable appetite for Next. By the end of the first season, we had sixty-five shops up and running.

Phyllis's well-organized PR campaign had played a major part in attracting customers to our doors. But in the end I believe it was the shop and the product that proved Next's strongest marketing assets. Here you had a brand-new chain of stores, merchandised with stylish clothes at accessible prices – *the affordable collectables* as we tagged the concept in *Vogue*. Everything about our High Street image was upmarket, from the shop fittings to the salesgirls, who were dressed in Next merchandise and looked wonderful. Everything, that is, bar the prices. The PR campaign certainly raised consumer awareness at the outset, but thereafter it was the Next formula that kept people coming back. As we developed, so the need for us actively to seek publicity diminished. We became involved in sponsorship, notably in the world of show-jumping, but we never felt that there was a need for massive PR and advertising campaigns. Before the launch of Next, I'd been advised by

Professor Channon from the Manchester Business School that you couldn't launch a business like ours without spending between £3m and £4m on advertising. I think we got away with £100,000. And in later years, our advertising expenditure was so negligible that it didn't even feature in management accounts. In this, as in many other aspects of our business our method was highly unconventional. But effective.

The incredible response to our first season's sixty-five shops didn't prevent me from having nagging doubts about the future. We'd done it the first time round, but was that not simply due to a combination of luck and the novelty factor? Could we sustain and build upon our early success, or were we simply a one-off wonder?

Our Autumn season was due to start that Summer of 1982, and four new shops, in Huntingdon, Waltham Cross, Hempstead Valley and Sheffield, would be opening on 4th August. That morning I set off very early for the Huntingdon store with our Sales Director, Alan MacNeil. The shop appeared to be doing reasonably good business, but when I began talking to one of the salesgirls, who'd come to us from Marks and Spencer, I discovered that our cash systems were at best antiquated and at worst a threat to the business. The girl explained that she had only a drawer for taking cash. I confess that I hadn't been much involved in the sales systems of our operation, but I could now see that although we had excellent merchandise and a fresh image, we were very lax behind the scenes. I got straight on the phone, and ordered 100 Sanyo tills.

The day had got off to a bad start, and somewhat discouraged, we motored on down to Waltham Cross in Hertfordshire. My first thought as we arrived was, 'This is not a Next town.' And sure enough, we entered the shop to discover that although it was gone midday, total takings were a mere £16. We travelled on to Hempstead Valley, which is in Kent, arriving at the Next store in the late afternoon. It was situated in a downmarket Savacentre, and once again, I couldn't help feeling that we weren't going to find many Next customers around here. And I was right: the shop had taken £64, and although it stayed open until 9 p.m. that first day, its total takings were still only £95 by closing time. When you consider that new stores had been taking a daily average of £400 in our first season, you can begin to understand why I felt depressed. My mood wasn't improved when I returned with Alan to our hotel, and phoned Sheffield to discover how they had done. I remember walking down to the bar to find Alan afterwards. 'Well?' he asked me. 'It's the same story,' I replied gloomily. '£26. I think the bubble's burst.'

We consoled ourselves with several pints before retiring to our rooms. As I lay in bed, I thought through the day and tried to work out where we'd gone wrong. By the morning I felt more positive: if things go wrong in business, there's no point in sitting back and accepting defeat. You have to go out on the attack. I got up at 5 a.m. and called Phyllis Walters. I told her that we'd been too complacent and that now we needed some PR to get these new shops off the ground. I wanted her suggestions within the hour.

The Right Sites

Of course PR wasn't the whole answer to the problem. The purchase of Kendalls had provided us with seventy-eight shops, most of which were very well-situated for our purpose. Inevitably, these would have to be supplemented by further sites as Next expanded, and the Huntingdon, Waltham Cross, Hempstead Valley and Sheffield stores were among these new purchases. Trevor Morgan did a brilliant job in acquiring the original Next portfolio of sites, but some of the newer sites, whilst being excellent acquisitions from a property criteria – low rents, good leases etc., were still not totally right for Next. They would have been ideal for Turners, a low-price shoe shop chain bought by Hepworths. Perhaps Trevor's approach was a legacy of his days as MD at Turners, a low price shoe-shop chain, bought by Hepworths back in May 1980. After all, Turners had always done exceedingly well in places like Waltham Cross. But Turners was downmarket, and Next was not. My suspicions that our problems with these new stores stemmed from Trevor's choice of sites were confirmed by the sales figures that began to come in from the stores we'd opened back in February, and which were part of the original Kendalls' purchase: they – unlike the new stores – were all continuing to trade very well.

You can be the best retailer in the world, but if you set up your shop in the wrong place, you'll never do much business. If you operate from the wrong properties, you start with your hands tied behind your back. Trevor's new sites were cheap, and they were cheap for two very good reasons. The first was that he had chosen the wrong towns. When I'd originally been asked where we should look for our new sites, I'd replied, 'Wherever the Tory voters are.' It may have seemed a peculiar reply, and I remember being laughed at by the Hepworths' people, but the point I was making was that *you should always go where your customer is*, and not be guided solely by the rental of your shop. Unlike Trevor, I wasn't an expert in property, but I knew where I wanted our shops. Waltham Cross was not the home of the Next customer, so even though it was relatively cheap, it was a complete non-starter as far as we were concerned. Scarborough, Andover and Torquay were other towns that were never quite right for Next, and which we either closed down or turned into Next-to-Nothing stores. It's far better in business to admit failure and cut your losses as soon as you can, rather than to let poor performers drain your profits. Huntingdon, the first place I'd visited that depressing day, presented a similar problem: it was wrong for us, because it was a secondary town. We should have been in Cambridge, which was down the road, but we had opted for Huntingdon because it was cheaper.

Our experience at Sheffield illustrates the second reason why the new sites were cheap. Unlike the towns I mentioned, Sheffield was absolutely right for Next, but the store was off the beaten track in a place called Chapel Walk, by no means a prime pitch. In fact the Sheffield site performed very badly in its first week, but within a three-month period it was hitting the £10,000 a week mark. So although Chapel Walk had seemed an unlikely location to begin with, it actually proved to be one of Trevor's most brilliant buys. That store taught me that as long as you have the right town, you can do very well with an off-pitch site. You just have to back it up with some PR (which Phyllis did in this case) and accept that it's going to take a little longer to take off.

I soon became heavily involved with the property aspects of the business. Trevor would step down from Next in May of 1983 – as he had always intended – so it was quite natural that I should assume the task of finding further properties along with Jeremy Dexter, from Hepworths' property department. The more I learned about the property world, the more I realized that like retailing, it's a market that's always on the move. I'll never forget the case of our Sunderland store, which I throught would prove an excellent site because it was situated on the High Street. The trouble was that although the street was still *called* the High Street, all the shops had now moved to a new precinct, so the High Street had, in effect, gone. If, as a retailer, you have pitched your shop on that High Street, you are still going to be paying an inflated High Street rent, even though the trade is no longer there. I know re-tailers who are bleeding to death because they are paying rents of £70,000, and yet taking only £2,000 a week.

At the other end of the scale there are pitches which are highly popu-lar, such as Oxford Street, simply because they attract so much passing trade. In those early days we deliberately avoided Oxford Street. It's so busy, and the demand for space there has resulted in phenomenally high rents. And there is also the matter of key money which is basically an 'entry fee' to the site, and can be as much as £1,000,000 for a small property. The more you rely on passing trade, the more you're going to pay in rent, irrespective of what the passing trade compromises. As far as Next was concerned, the sheer volume of people wasn't a good enough reason to move to Oxford Street. We knew who we were trying to reach, and we didn't want to pay for the privilege of crowds of people, most of whom weren't our potential customers. As we expanded in London we began to choose sites like those we developed in the City – not only did these offer us a high concentration of what I call 'our people', but because nobody else could see the value of the space, the rents were also relatively cheap.

The pressure on retailing space has led in recent years to the de-velopment of scores of American-style shopping malls, where rents are always expensive. The assumption that the traffic of customers will be high, combined with the chronic shortage of alternative space means that the developers can command whatever price they wish. For the big names in retailing, a mall pitch can work out very well, but if you're a small retailer, desperate for space, the overheads can be crippling. All the more so if the mall fails to perform as expected – and this happens all too frequently. The new shopping scheme in Birmingham is the classic example of a shopping mall that's run into difficulties. I'd had some reservations about the development when Next originally considered moving there in 1987 and I insisted on a corner pitch which fronted on to the High Street. As a result, we haven't suffered from the mall's disappointing performance.

The demand for retailing space and the resulting rise in rents has meant that many retailers have begun to seek outlets other than the traditional store. In the case of Next, the hunt for alternative outlets was also prompted by pressure from the City to keep up our rate of growth. These two factors were instrumental in our development into what I would call the 'complete' store, the Next Directory and the 24-hour shop.

However, there was much to be done before we would move in those directions. The business continued to grow, with new shops opening all over the country, and in July 1983 I was appointed on to the Hepworths' Main Board as Group Retail MD. My responsibilities now included the Hepworths' men's wear range, which was to undergo a dramatic transformation, and as 1983 progressed, I found myself busier and under more stress than ever before. I have always thrived under pressure, but at this stage in my life there was an additional source of stress which was making things very difficult for me.

My Marriage to Liz

Liz Devereaux-Batchelor and I had always maintained a professional working relationship. I love women, and I suppose I am something of a flirt, but I'd known for a long time that you couldn't play games with Liz. She had made this very clear to me when at a Pippa Dee fashion show she had refused my invitation to dance. Liz was very correct and, like me, she was married. But over the years our friendship had grown and because of her ability, I had come to admire her and rely upon her. We had travelled together extensively on buying trips, but there had never been anything untoward about our dealings with one another. In the December of 1982, however, things changed between us. We were at the end of a fortnight-long buying trip to South Africa. It was our last night, and I vividly remember that we were sitting in the President Hotel in Cape Town, quietly having a drink, when I made a light-hearted comment along the lines of, 'You've never really liked me on a personal basis, have you?', jokingly referring to her refusal to dance with me all those years ago. Liz looked at me and said, 'Oh no, you've got it completely wrong.' As our eyes met, I suddenly saw before me a completely different person, and in those few seconds my life and hers changed irrevocably.

We returned home and worked together for the next few weeks rather like a pair of kids. I was excited by my feelings for Liz, but also very fearful because I knew that this was serious: I had found the person with whom I wanted to spend the rest of my life. I suggested to Liz that we meet up in London three or four days after we got back from South Africa, and she said that she couldn't without telling Mac, her husband.

When she did tell him a few weeks later, I wondered for a while if my number was up. We were returning from a trip to Germany in the New Year, and Liz had called her husband to tell him she wouldn't be coming home. As we arrived at Birmingham airport, we spotted Mac with a very large male companion. Mac grabbed Liz and whisked her off to his car, and I was left with the other fellow. I had no means of getting to Leicester, and perhaps out of nervousness, I turned to the man, introduced myself by name and asked him if he could give me a lift home. He looked rather taken aback – I think he'd probably come to 'look after me' in quite a different manner. But he led me to his car, and even offered me a cigarette as he drove me home. I wasn't a smoker but I accepted nonetheless!

I had married my first wife Anne while I was still very young – 23 – and now that I had fallen in love with Liz, I could see the difficulties of that first marriage. Anne and I had rowed terribly for years, but it was still very hard to break away after eighteen years, especially because we had three daughters. I left home for a couple of months, but then returned in the Spring of 1983 in an attempt to patch up my family life. It must have been a very difficult time for Liz. In the end, however, I knew that I had to leave. I talked the decision through with my two elder daughters, Melanie and Emma – Alex, the youngest, was only ten at the time. They were traumatic times. The divorce took a long time to come through. I believe in loyalty, and I was never able to reconcile that belief with my behaviour towards Anne. It remains one of the saddest chapters of my life. After the break-up of my marriage, my priority was to remain in close contact with my daughters. Today they live six miles from me, and I see them all frequently.

Liz and I were finally able to marry in the December of 1985. She understands my world completely and is my mentor and friend. She is a tremendously capable person and has great stamina. The latter was commented upon in the *Times* City Diary, early in June this year, when Liz gave birth to our second daughter, Jessica. She had actually worked until late the night before the birth; we had gone into hospital about eight hours after she'd left work, and 1½ hours later, Jessica was born! Liz also has one of the finest design senses of our time, and has taught me much about flair and style. While I can see what the consumer wants, and can predict trends for the future, it's Liz who chooses the right colour and refines my ideas down to design and product. Without her, Next could never have been the success that it was.

Giving Hepworths The Next Treatment

My promotion to Group Retail MD in July 1983 was the result of some months of discussions about Hepworths' future. In the Autumn of 1982 they'd adopted a policy of converting some of the stores to improve the Hepworth image, and I believe some £20,000 was spent on each store conversion. As far as I was concerned, it was wasted money, because there is little point in changing the shop unless you are also going to change the product. Trevor Morgan had become involved in this project, in an effort to help the Hepworth buying team become conversant with the Next formula, thereby influencing their men's wear range. The trouble was that they couldn't understand the complex mix of ingredients that had made Next what it was. Our greatest strength was that we were a tight team of people with complementary skills, and because our work was entirely product led, nothing – not even the building of our prototype shop – was done without the involvement of our product people. How then could they possibly copy our formula without changing Hepworths' merchandise? And how could they change the merchandise without Liz and the rest of my team? Trevor and I had many debates during this period, and I remember him saying to me on one occasion, 'The trouble is, George, that while I want evolution for Hepworths, you want revolution.' How right he was.

By the summer of 1983, the revamped Hepworths stores still hadn't achieved their hoped-for results, and with my promotion I was handed the task of giving Hepworths the Next treatment. My arrival on the Board came shortly after a number of other major changes at senior level. Terence Conran had relinquished his Chairmanship that May, principally because of his growing commitments to the Habitat-Mothercare group. He was succeeded by Deputy Chairman Michael Stoddart. I remember one amusing incident involving Terence and Michael, while Terence was still Chairman. We'd all arrived for a meeting at Terence's Deal Street offices in London. When Michael Stoddart arrived, Terence remarked to him, 'Do you think you are dressed correctly for the Deputy Chairman of a company aspiring to sartorial elegance?' In his rush to dress that morning, Stoddart had put on the navy jacket of one suit, and the grey trousers of another! Mike was normally impeccably turned out.

Soon after his resignation from the Board, Terence put in an informal offer for Hepworths – he was clever enough to see that we were about to embark upon a new phase of development, and that Next was going to be a major force to reckon with in retailing. Roger Seelig from Morgan Grenfell (now a close friend and adviser) and a man called Ian Peacock, the Habitat-Mothercare Finance Director, came and made a presentation to us. Afterwards, Michael Stoddart went round the table, asking each of us what we thought of the proposal. Everyone, it seemed, was impressed and felt that the least we could do was inform our shareholders.

I took a different view, however, and in this I was supported by our Finance Director, Gerry McLeod. I opposed the bid, for I believed we were running the Group well and that we needed no outside intervention. I recognised that a takeover would have boosted the price of the shares in the short term. But I believed that Terence's bid was wrong for the company, and that in the long term we would serve our shareholders far better. As at Pippa Dee, I was prepared to uphold this belief even if it meant the loss of my job. After much debate we decided to call in our merchant banker and advisers, Kleinwort Benson. Their man Holland-Bosworth supported Gerry McLeod and me against Michael Stoddart. He said that we had no obligation whatsoever to go to the shareholders, and that if we felt we could carry on alone, then that's what we should do. I knew very little about the workings of the City at the time, but this incident helped me to have a far better understanding and confidence in my own views where the City was involved. No one Board member can have all the answers.

The matter ended there, and very shortly afterwards (in October 1983), Terence bought Richard Shops from the Hanson Trust, with the backing of Morgan Grenfell. I couldn't help but remember a conversation we'd had just before he resigned from the Board of Hepworths. Terence had said to me that he was leaving so that he could compete with us, and I'd replied that I'd welcome the competition. I did. It now seemed inappropriate that we should work with any part of the Conran Group, and we reached a mutual decision to part company with Conran's advertising arm, which was our remaining connection with the Group.

As Hepworth Group Retail MD I was now responsible for the 350 Hepworths' stores. I knew there were problems, but now that I was directly involved in the business, I could see that the chain was in a dreadful mess. They were carrying more than a year's stock, and their merchandising was in a state of utter chaos. Regent Street, one of their prime sites, was doing less than £30,000; when it became a Next store the figure was to rise to over £100,000 in our first week. If they were taking £60m a year in the Hepworth men's wear chain and running the show so inefficiently I was sure I could do a lot better. Rather than make hasty decisions, I decided to go up to Leeds for several weeks with Liz and Colin Shiner, our Merchandise Manager who'd worked with me at Littlewoods and Pippa Dee, and had now come on board at Next. We would work with Hepworths people, assess the situation and then find a solution.

It didn't take me very long to see that I was going to have to centralize our retailing operation – I couldn't commute between Kendalls in Leicester and Hepworths in Leeds. Fortunately we had recently acquired the necessary office and warehousing space at our new Next headquarters in Enderby. The decrepit Kendalls building was never going to house our burgeoning business for very long, and by a stroke of luck the UDS fashion chain, Van Allen, had closed down and vacated its purpose-built headquarters in Enderby – just outside Leicester. We had moved in.

A further reason for wishing to get everyone under the same roof was that Hepworths simply didn't have the talent I needed for a visionary new approach to men's wear. I would have to use my ladies' wear team. I'd looked at a variety of men's wear chains – Dunns, Fentons, Colliers as well as Hepworths – and I'd seen that everyone was turning out the same drab and uninspiring merchandise. The clothes were very traditional and without any of the stylishness the Italians, say, were producing. In London there were one or two expensive shops like Paul Smith and Woodhouse, where stylish garments were being sold. But elsewhere, there was nothing other than Top Man, which catered only for the young, and besides wasn't an upmarket operation. To look at the High Street, one would have thought that British men were congenitally staid, and without any interest whatsoever in fashion.

When you are confronted with a situation of this sort, you have to ask yourself why it is that people keep coming up with the same tired old formulae? It's easy to assume that it's a response to consumer demand, but in this case, nothing could have been further from the truth. British men had grown out of the conservatism of the post-war years; they now had the confidence and freedom to experiment with fashion, but most of them were unable to afford the stylish garments that were beginning to appear in Paul Smith etc. And for those living outside London, there wasn't even that option. So the men's wear trade wasn't reacting to consumer demand at all, it was sluggishly perpetuating years of stuffy and ill-fitting tradition. I discovered that the source of all of this was in the very structure of the business: while the women's wear trade had developed a dynamism of its own, its opposite number was run by old, or older-thinking, men, who hadn't the desire or the ability to react to changing fashions. The manufacturers, the agents, the buyers – they were all the same, and while the old order remained intact, there was little chance of change. And there was no male fashion press – the elderly press barons had no interest in clothes either. I realized that the only way I could revitalize men's wear was to bring in my female buyers, who had experience of the dynamism of the ladies' wear market. It was time to ring the changes.

One of the first things I tackled was Hepworths' misguided advertising campaign. One of the advertisements featured a couple of men, the first in a flash tie and check jacket, the second in a suit. The copy asked women which of the pair they'd prefer, and of course the answer was supposed to be the smart fellow in the grey suit. But the funny thing was that I kept receiving letters from women who wanted the name and address of the *other* man! So the campaign was clearly misfiring!

Them and Us

I was never going to make myself popular at the Hepworths' building – I was up-ending years of tradition. Maybe that's why so few of the Hepworths' people decided to come with us when the move happened. Ours was a totally different culture – the pace was different, the style of management was different and, of course, we had female buyers. I think that in the chauvinistic men's wear world, many of the men from Hepworths simply couldn't reconcile themselves to the notion of women in positions of authority. How they must have seethed when they learned that we actually had women selling in the menswear stores! I remember offering a job at Enderby to the Hepworths' Merchandise Director, a man called Jonathan Parker. After three months, he decided to leave, presumably because the environment did not suit him. Many of the Hepworth's team did not suit our requirements, but of those who did, very few took the jobs offered to them.

In a way I was not too disappointed because it meant that I could now start afresh with my team, most of whom were women and who weren't, therefore, indoctrinated by the old practices. Liz and Bob Williams moved over from Next ladies' wear, and they were joined by Frances Mossman, who came from Sabre – the knitwear chain – at the recommendation of Priscilla Conran, Terence's sister. Frances was highly talented, and proved an invaluable asset to the team. She and her husband Andrew – who would later join Next to take charge of acquisitions and mergers – were to become very dear friends of Liz and myself, and would prove their loyalty when we were sacked from Next. Colin Shiner was also on the new men's wear team; we'd originally brought him into the Group to help transform the fortunes of Turners, the shoe store chain, but with the sale of the company in early 1983, he'd suddenly found himself without a job. I didn't want his talent to go to waste, and brought him over to men's wear. We'd worked together over many years, and had a wonderful rapport, so it was good to have him on board once more.

I cannot emphasize enough the importance of teamwork at the beginning of a project. As I have explained I get my ideas from going out and about and digging up the grass root opinions, but the picture that then emerges is sharpened up and developed by the team. I need those people around me to transform my idea into a design. I've never been a designer, and I would never pretend to be. I'll go to my team, and describe my feeling, we'll then discuss it and they'll start to work on designs. This teamwork is never easy to achieve. If it were, every other shop on the High Street would be as successful as Next.

There were plenty of other difficulties to contend with. We had to run down the old Hepworths' lines, picking off certain shops as we went in preparation for the launch of *Next for men* in the August of 1984, and we still had some of the Hepworths' buyers on board who put pressure on us to continue in their old ways. An early battle was over Hepworths' determination to discontinue its made-to-measure service, which seemed paradoxical, given the character of their business! When I was in my twenties that was the way you bought your suit, but with the advent of large retailing chains, ready-to-wear suits took over from the bespoke tailors. Hepworths' reaction to the situation was to close down their old made-to-measure factories, with the subsequent loss of many, many jobs. When I arrived the last of these factories, which was in Ashington, was about to go. 500 workers would be made redundant.

I come from Liverpool, a depressed area where large manufacturers like Tate and Lyle had closed down factories over the years, rendering hundreds of people jobless, and I felt that we as management had a responsibility to our workers.

They say that Liverpool's a violent place, that it's run down and dangerous. But where does that process of disintegration start? I believe passionately that we must build a world with a social conscience, and that the 'we' must include the heads of business and industry. Management cannot shrug off lightly its responsibilites to its workers, merely because times have changed. We have to find ways in which we can use our people, and not simply pull out, decimating whole communities. Isn't there a more creature approach to the problem? I think so. I believed that made-to-measure was still a good concept, but that nobody had tried to bring it up to date.

At Hepworths we were still offering the customer a choice of perhaps 400 cloths, which was no longer necessary. It simply served to confuse. The quality of the suits wasn't up to much either. If we could reduce the choice of cloths to about seventy and then raise the quality of the product and the price, we would create an exclusive line for which there would be a demand. It was simply a matter of aligning an old – but good – idea with the times.

I persuaded the Hepworths' Board to give the Ashington factory a stay of execution. They agreed although I believe it was only beause they were worried about the redundancy costs they would incur – I learned this from Gerry McLeod, the Finance Director at the time and a personal friend of mine. The relaunch of Hepworths' made-to-measure Premier Club service in March 1984 proved a tremendous success, and it would continue to be so under the umbrella of *Next for men*. The Hepworth Board had thought Ashington had no future, but we'd proved them wrong: the factory became one of Next's most successful and it currently employs more than 500 people.

Many of the Hepworths shops I'd inherited were loss-making – especially the larger ones. Their sites ranged from 1,000 square feet right up to a massive 6 or 7,000 square feet. There was a move to get rid of these large stores where, naturally, the rents were much higher and which were tending not to pay their way. I was worried, for it seemed to me a retrograde step which we could come to regret as we expanded. Necessity is the mother of invention, and it was at this point that the whole vision of the 'complete' Next shop – a mini-department store – started to form in my mind.

As a first step along the way I decided to experiment by putting together our ladies' wear and men's wear ranges under a single roof. That's how the joint Next/Hepworth stores in Reading and Romford came about in the April of 1984. At Reading, we moved the men's wear upstairs, on to the first floor, and had Next on the ground floor. Men's wear had been taking £7,000 a week, but now that we had refitted the store, and brought in ladies' wear, takings rose to £11,000. Ladies' wear, at the same time, was taking £15,000. So on the same site we were now taking £26,000 a week as opposed to £7,000.

The received belief had always been that you couldn't band together a ladies' wear and men's wear store. It was one of the many rules we were to break, successfully, at Next.

Before the Reading and Romford stores opened, we had to enter into some tough negotiations with the trade unions. All the salesmen at Hepworths were members of USDAW – it was a closed shop – and the senior management had been paranoid about the set-up for years. Whenever we made suggestions such as keeping the shop open longer, or introducing some sort of bonus scheme (as we had at Next), the Hepworths' old guard would always back away, declaring that the union wouldn't allow it. In many ways, I can't help feeling that it was simply an excuse for not taking action. The other major bone of contention was wage increases: the unions would demand 11%, management would offer 3% and they'd end up compromising on 7%, which was a lot of money and bore no relation to profits. I remember asking the Hepworths' Board if they had ever *spoken* to any of the union officials, and I was a little surprised to find that they hadn't.

When I was appointed to the Main Board, I decided that the only way we would resolve this problem would be by facing up to the unions and discussing our differences with them. At the moment we had a non-unionized sales staff at Next, where I had built up a team whose loyalties were with the company, and a closed shop situation at Hepworths. They were two different cultures, and more crucially, without breaking the closed shop agreement we wouldn't be able to go ahead with our plans to join Next and Hepworths under a single roof.

I'd had no union involvement before, but I arranged to meet Terry Sullivan, an USDAW National Officer, and this was followed by further discussions with Bill Whatley, the General Secretary. We had a reasonable chat, where I explained our problem. I told USDAW that it would be in their members' interests to end the closed shop agreement. Next, the non-unionized part of our business, was growing and creating jobs every day, while Hepworths' record was of closure and redundancy. I explained that I couldn't invest in the men's wear business, and transform it, as I had transformed Kendalls, if my hands were going to be tied by union regulations. I wasn't a union knocker, and I had a vision of creating a cooperative environment where the unions played an active part in our business – they would function more along the lines of an advisory service, where we could enter into creative dialogue. One of the suggestions I put forward was that *everyone* in the Group should become a union member – including myself. After all, I was as much an employee as anybody else, and I couldn't and didn't feel as though I 'owned' the staff, because I was involved day in day out with my team in the front line of our business. We were all part of one team. We discussed the possibility of perhaps having some sort of company subscription, with contributions of 50p a week per person.

The other issue we discussed was the inevitable closure of Hepworths' stores. Although the larger ones would become part of our big store plan, there were a few small stores in towns which didn't suit our customer profile and which we'd have to close – Tonbridge, Haverford West and Fort William are three that come to mind. Some of the managers had served with us for twenty years, and it seemed grossly unjust simply to pat them on the back and then send them off to redundancy or early retirement. Such matters need to be approached with sensitivity and understanding, and our plan – and this is what we eventually did – was to offer every manager the possibility of buying his shop. We tried to see the union point of view on all matters.

I think it's a great pity that the trade union movement in this country has failed to keep itself up to date with the changing times. Bill Whatley could see the sense of what we were saying; these were constructive ideas, in British terms far ahead of their time. Initially he was keen to carry through our idea about membership for the whole group, but in the end he admitted that he would never convince his colleagues at General Council. However his sympathy to our approach to labour relations did clear the way for the breaking of the closed shop and we were now able to go ahead with our plans for the Reading and Romford stores.

We had further discussions with the trade unions over transport arrangements. For years Hepworths had used a fleet of their own, which was a TGWU closed shop. The problem for me was that they weren't as efficient as I would have liked: they worked a strict Monday to Friday, which meant that our stores weren't getting replenished at the weekend. We set up a series of talks whereby we were able to change the balance and create a new working rota which included Saturday and Sunday. Hepworths' management had never confronted these problems, just accepting the status quo. I think the main reason for *our* success with the unions was that they could see we were growing and that that would mean more jobs for their people.

I had spoken to Bill Whatley at USDAW about setting up constructive dialogue between management and workers, and it now seemed to me that an in-house staff council would create the right forum for that sort of discussion, particularly over the issue of wage increases. But what really prompted me to take action on this front was some trouble that blew up among our warehousing staff several months later. I first realized that we had a problem as I was sitting in my office. I heard a terrible commotion coming from the warehouse. I rushed outside to discover that we had a picket at our gate, and a strike on our hands. The discontent had brewed among a few new recruits to the TGWU, who were members of our warehousing staff, and who were seeking recognition of their rights as union members. Seven of them, who worked a twenty-four-hour rota, were picketing our gates with banners and posters. We'd had very little trouble with our staff until then, but now we were confronted with a crisis. There was some very negative local press coverage which was demoralizing, but worse than that was the real threat to our business that this small band of men represented. All merchandise passed through the central warehouse, and if the picket successfully stopped our trucks from coming through the gates, our flow of stock would quickly dry up. We were especially worried that one of our key delivery contractors, who were also TGWU members, would refuse to cross the picket lines. Stuart Rowland, who was managing our warehousing and distribution, had secret talks with the union representatives of Tibbett and Britten, and explained that the strike was not about pay (as they had assumed) but about union recognition. They agreed thereafter to carry on with business.

But even if some contractors agreed to cross their lines we still had pickets on the gate, so our problem was by no means resolved. I decided that the only thing to do would be to go and have a chat with the men and try to discover the exact nature of their grievances. I went outside and suggested to one of them that we go over to the pub for a quick drink. There I discovered that there were several legitimate sources of tension, all of which had their roots in poor man management. The men were expected to be on call twenty-four hours a day, and yet they might not hear until 6 p.m. that they would have to work that night. Furthermore, the night shift got no more pay than the day shift workers, which was clearly unfair. It's all these important small things which niggle away at people and make them feel put upon – and that's bad management. The upshot of this informal meeting was that we held a vote to discover if the non-unionized warehousing staff wanted to be represented by the TGWU – by a majority of one, they voted against unionization. I can't say that I wasn't relieved. As for our strikers, we looked at their complaints and resolved our differences. They'd shown me that I had to be wary about the insensitivity of some of my managers, and that we really did need somewhere for staff to air their grievances. And that's how our staff councils came about.

In a sense they provided a way of binding together the two cultures of Next and Hepworths, thus easing the transition of the men's wear staff in to *Next for men*. They were also a safety valve. Representatives from every part of our business were elected on to one of the two councils we set up (the first for sales people, and the second for office and warehouse staff). I remember that one of our early discussions was about wage increases. I suggested that as these were due very shortly, perhaps council members should start thinking about what sort of rise they thought was the right one. Some of them – especially those with union backgrounds – were immediately suspicious, convinced that this was some sort of management con. It was so unconventional that it had to be a trick! We stuck to the proposal, however, explaining that there was no point in simply plucking a percentage out of the air. What we had to do first of all was look at how our wages compared with those of other retailers. We then had to consider inflation and also how much the company could actually afford. On that occasion, I believe we gave rises to the order of 15%, because we discovered that our staff were slightly less well-paid than staff in comparable retailing organizations. But the following year, wages were upped by 4½%, because inflation was just below that level.

Exercises of this nature proved very positive, because they involved our people at all levels in the business. The staff councils developed into a powerful force for good, where we would discuss not only wages but ideas for selling and so forth, and they played a vital role in creating the Next culture. When we purchased Grattans in 1986, the challenge was to incorporate their people into our staff councils and, indeed, any other of the activities in which our people were involved. Some people did not like change or any attempt to join together our two businesses. I firmly believe that it was imperative to do this and to create a culture that would amalgamate the qualities and strengths of both sides into a new Next.

Many a business has foundered as a result of labour relations. Too few British managers have ever learned how to bridge the divide between management and workers. Perhaps I was at an advantage, because my background wasn't establishment and in many ways I associated myself with the workers. In any case, I refused to adopt the 'them' and 'us' attitude that is so prevalent. As far as I was concerned, we all shared the common aim of building the business. When I used to do the rounds of the Next stores, I would often suggest to the staff that we pop out for a drink together if it was the end of the day – that was my style, and I loved it. I think that many of my senior managers might have found this hard to cope with, and it must have come as quite a shock to those bred in the Hepworths' corporate style, which was quite different from the one we would develop at Next. Management is about consensus, not confrontation – I'd learned that during my days at Pippa Dee.

Next For Men

The last of the Hepworths' stores was phased out in the summer of 1985. Some 300 stores had been redesigned, remerchandised and transformed into *Next for men*, which was launched on 16 August 1984. The success of the Next ladies' wear concept had proven that 'revolution' and not 'evolution' was the only way in which to turn around the fortunes of our men's wear range. My team and I were given a free hand to develop the concept.

A key player in this process was Katrina Ellis, a highly talented designer whom I'd originally met at Conran Design. Tina – as she was known – was very largely responsible for the successful formula developed for the ladies' wear stores, and we'd always had a marvellous rapport. Of course, the Conran Group was no longer involved with Next, but as Tina had since left them to have a baby, I phoned her at home to see if she could work on a design concept for the *Next for Men* stores. We'd contracted a design consultancy called the Jenkins Group to do the work, but I felt that Tina was the person to whom I could best communicate my ideas. The concept she and the Jenkins Group came up with remains, I believe, one of Next's best. I wanted a look that combined the contemporary with the traditional, and the result was both stylish and masculine, but not so masculine as to make the female shopper feel uncomfortable. The look has been copied by many other retailers, and I believe it has stood the test of time better than the ladies' wear stores. Exceptional design doesn't date.

The launch of *Next for Men* was far less of a nerve-racking affair than our ladies' wear launch back in 1982. Our first store was in South Molton Street, and that opening day it took £10,800. Once more, we eschewed TV advertising, because we wanted to create an aura of exclusivity which TV would have destroyed. As with the earlier launch, we selected a few publications in which we advertised mostly in the sport and City pages. We also took the PR route that Phyllis Walters had led us down in the early days: there was a series of articles in national and provincial papers; a spread in *Vogue* wasn't paid for this time, as it was editorial copy. The whole operation was very much easier, as we were now a known and respected force in the fashion world. Sadly, Phyllis Walters and I had fallen out that Spring, just before the opening of the first *Next for Men* stores. There had been various difficulties between us, but I suppose what brought matters to a head was our failure to come to any agreement over Phyllis's contract now that we had men's wear as well as the original concept to promote. She had done some marvellous things for Next, and was largely responsible for the success of our launch, but the company was growing and developing a team culture with which she couldn't identify. I had learnt the techniques of PR, and now led our new campaign with Annie Sharp, the new Press Officer, who had come from managing our Cheapside store.

A month before the men's wear launch, I was appointed joint Group MD with Jeff Rowlay. Six months later – in January 1985 – he would retire and I would become Group Chief Executive. When I look back now, I identify Trevor Morgan as the man who encouraged more than any other my progress up the ranks at Hepworths. For that I am very grateful. Trevor and I always had a bit of a love-hate relationship, and often we had violent disagreements. But I owe him a very great deal: it was he who bought Kendalls, he who recruited me and allowed me to bring my team. As MD of Kendalls in those early days, Trevor took the pressure from the Hepworths' Board, thus giving me the freedom to develop the Next concept. Once we were up and running, he had the grace to step down from Next and move back over to Hepworths, so that I could carry on with my work. More than anyone. I'd like to give him the credit for the launch of Next.

Unhappily Trevor died in sad circumstances. The last time I saw him was at Liz's and my wedding in December 1985. He'd had some personal difficulties and had taken an overdose from which he'd recovered a couple of weeks before. He seemed to be overcoming his depression, but then a few months later we heard that he'd hanged himself from a tree in his garden.

7

STYLISH
MANAGEMENT

Our Extraordinary Culture

Our rate of growth had been phenomenal. In August of 1981 – the year I joined Hepworths – the group had announced profits of £4 million. But by August 1983, the figure had risen to £8.6m. With the improved Hepworths men's wear range and subsequent arrival of *Next for men*, we were able to announce profits of £13.6m in 1984. Share prices rose accordingly, and continued to do so in the years to follow. It was an extraordinary growth curve that made us the darlings of the City. Having witnessed, and reaped the benefits of our performance, the institutions based their predictions for our future on our impressive past. Up to a certain point, we were able to rise to each new challenge, announcing profits each year that satisfied the high expectations of the City and of the commentators. But there came a time when we had to slow down, and that's when I fell from grace. After my firing, John Erdman, a retail expert at Morgan Stanley in New York, was to say to me that I had dug my own grave: in providing such a steep growth curve in the early years of Next, I had given rise to the sort of expectations that nobody would have been able to fulfil.

The heady years of 1984 and '85 were wonderful times, and although I can honestly say that hardly a day has gone by in my life that I haven't enjoyed, those years leading up to the January of 1986 remain among the best. They were certainly the happiest years I would spend at Next. It's hard to beat the exhilaration of creating, launching and developing a new business: there was plenty of fear, and one or two disappointments, but the prevailing moods were of excitement and comradeship. The atmosphere at Enderby buzzed with purposefulness, and the commitment among staff at all levels was akin to a missionary zeal – the company car park was always full by 8 a.m. My day was a long one, starting with phone calls from 7.45 onwards, and it was often 11.30 p.m. before I left the office. But it was no longer than my secretary Anne James's day, nor that of many other Next people who shared my vision for the company, and were prepared to put in the hours in order to make that vision reality.

Nor did the hard work deter the queues of people who wanted to join Next and become part of our extraordinary culture. I particularly remember the case of David Wareing, who subsequently became Divisional Sales Manager for the North of England. David was originally turned down after an interview with Alan MacNeil the Sales Director, but he was so determined to join us that he cut a holiday short and persuaded us to see him again. I met him and decided on the spot to take him on board. David was one of our most dedicated people at Next, and when Liz and I were fired, he was among those who felt they couldn't remain at the company any longer.

When new people joined Next, you could watch their transformation as they became part of the team – it was incredible to observe how they would absorb the Next philosophy and emerge within a matter of days more stylish, and dedicated to the well-being of our company. At times I think we were rather like a religious sect! Our staff would go home and talk about Next, with the result that we would have mothers, brothers, sisters, husbands all wanting to join us – France Mossman's husband Andrew is only one, senior, example of the phenomenon. David Wareing's three daughters all worked for us at various stages and there were more cases across every part of the company.

We were a family in many ways, and the business was run without

Right: George Davies, aged
nine months
Below: England Schoolboys
Under 18 team. George
Davies aged 19 (front row,
far right)

Left: The window that changed the face of the high street

Above: Department X, Oxford Street (designed by Rasshied Din Associates)

Left: Next, Kensington High Street (designed by Rasshied Din Associates)

The co-ordinated look that was the cornerstone of Next's retailing philosophy

Top: Next Directory II
Espresso bar, Regent Street

Above: Co-ordinates

Margaret Thatcher opening the new Next offices at Enderby in 1987

Next Interiors

Quality and affordibility were of paramount importance to George Davies and Next.

Above: George and Liz at their wedding, with John Roberts as his best man. (photo Desmond O'Neill)

Right: George Davies was awarded an honorary Fellowship of the Royal College of Art in July 1988. (photo Frank Thurston)

George Davies at home with his family (1 to r, Liz and Jessica, Melanie, George and Lucia, Emma, Alex) (photo Neil Robinson)

any of the absurd corporate rules that so many other companies rely upon. At Hepworths they had a strict hierarchy, but at Next we had a different style of management which manifested itself in all sorts of little things. We all ate in the same canteen, for instance, and I would queue for my lunch along with everyone else, which I always enjoyed. If the queue was too long, I'd simply go away and return later – there was no preferential treatment for executives. Even when I was made Chairman and Chief Executive in October 1987 I continued to be known as 'George' by all the Next people, with the exception of Renée, our wonderful receptionist, who was quite a character and could never bring herself to call me anything other than 'Mr Davies'. On one occasion after my departure, I rang Next and Renée burst into tears on recognizing my voice.

The hard work at Next had its rewards, and I especially loved giving people surprises. There was a memorable occasion in Paris, where Liz and Frances Mossman had gone to attend the *Première Vision*, which is the first showing of the season's clothes. I was due to join them on the Friday, and that morning I suggested to Andrew Mossman, who was by this time General Manager of Next Directory, that he might come too. It was Frances's and his wedding anniversary, and we could give her a surprise.

I phoned Liz in Paris, letting her in on the secret, and arranging a rendez-vous at the hotel. When we arrived, however, they had gone to the hairdresser. We made our way over there with Claude, the driver we always used in Paris, picking up en route Georgia Baldini (a friend and supplier), so that we could carry on for dinner. Outside the hairdresser, Andrew quickly borrowed Claude's coat, wrapped a scarf around his neck, concealing most of his face in the process, donned a cap and jumped into the front beside Claude. Frances and Liz emerged looking sheepish, for we were late for our dinner booking. I pretended to be rather cool with them. 'Claude's brought his cousin,' I remarked, indicating Andrew's muffled figure. 'That's a bit cheeky, isn't it?' said Frances, trying hard to make amends and pulling a face at the "interloper". At this point, Andrew asked Claude. *'Ou est-ce qu'on va, mon cousin?'*, turning round as he spoke, and catching Frances grimacing behind his back. The look of utter disbelief on her face was quite unforgettable!

My management syle was based on a love of people. I get on with men and women from all walks of life, and I believe that one of my strengths is that I can break down the barriers which normally divide management from workers – I'd proved this in my dealings with the trades unions.

But perhaps I was not as shrewd a judge of character as I might have been: the recent painful times have taught me much more about people whom I had always previously thought were close to me. My affection and enthusiasm for individuals sometimes clouds my judgement – and Liz constantly reminds me of this weakness. I always made myself available to staff, whatever their position in the company, and people would come and talk to me quite freely. Whenever someone left the company, it was normal practice for them to pop in and say goodbye to me. I felt this informality was very important because it keeps you in touch with the heart of your business and gives you a more balanced approach to management decisions. I think that it's all too easy for chief executives of large corporations to lose touch with their business, and with hindsight I now see that I too lost touch with Next in the latter months. I was so involved in running this vast retailing operation that I failed to make time for many of my people.

At Next staff were promoted on merit. We didn't believe that because you were a secretary, a receptionist or whatever, you would necessarily remain so for the rest of your working life. If we saw that somebody was capable of more demanding work, then we promoted them to a position that exploited their talents – regardless of qualifications. There's an endless list of people whose lives were transformed by Next in this way: Sue Ricks, who came as a temp from Reed Employment, is now Senior Buyer on Accessories: Alan MacNeil, a Hepworths Junior Area Manager, became Group Sales Director; Peter Ward, an assistant in the shopfitting department at Hepworths, became our Shopfitting Director; Geoff Bunney, a stock controller, became Group Merchandise Director; and Jane Carver moved from sales assistant to Sales Director. Next gave all these people the opportunity to grow. We were less interested in qualifications than in raw talent, energy and a commitment to the company. Weak managers appoint the wrong people to the wrong jobs and then blame those people when they fail to perform, but at Next we majored on the talent of each individual and put that talent to work. The case of Sue Myatt illustrates this point. Sue was working as a rather indifferent Area Manager but when we moved her over to display, she blossomed and she's now Group Display Director.

So many people simply don't know their own potential because they've never been guided into the right job. I believe there's a bit of a conspiracy among those in positions of power, who like to maintain their power by holding others back – it's a form of self-protection, I suppose. I've always likened the management of staff to that of a football team, where everyone has a part to play, and where the trick is to get each player into the position where he can display his talent. A natural goalkeeper doesn't need to be able to run fast, but he must have quick hands and reflexes, and a natural centre forward needs nimble feet and good acceleration, but need not be able to catch a ball to save his life. If the pair find themselves in the wrong positions, they will both perform badly, but once they are in place they'll win you the match. It's the same in business: the art of good management is to identify people who are in the wrong job, and to convert them – as it were – from a poor goalkeeper into a first class centre forward. The result is not only a happy and fulfilled staff, but also increased productivity.

There were many ways in which we created the strong corporate identity that was Next's. Apart from the staff council which I've already written about, the other major vehicle for bringing together our people was the six-monthly conference, the concept of which I had brought with me from Pippa Dee. At these conferences we would have a fashion show so that everyone could see the new ranges, followed by what we called our Merit Award Ceremony. As at Pippa Dee, these occasions were always tremendous fun for everybody, but they also made people think about the company as a whole, its goals, and where they – as individuals – might contribute to those common goals. We would all leave those conferences with a renewed pride in Next, and an increased determination to keep on building the company.

Some of our conferences took the form of garden parties. We had one at Woburn, another at Leeds Castle and another at Blenheim. The latter I remember in particular, because the day before the conference was wet and blustery, with a gale force eight wind which threatened to carry away the marquee. But when the next day dawned we awoke to a brilliant blue sky. Someone must have been smiling upon us, for throughout my seven years at Next we didn't have a single drop of rain at those garden parties. The biggest extravaganza of them all took place in the July of 1987, at Stanford Hall – a stately home about fifteen miles from Next headquarters. Having presented our Merit Awards we led everyone off to a further marquee which was set up to look like an amphitheatre with a semi-circle of seating opening on to a lake. The fashion show started, with the models appearing out of the darkness from an island and crossing the water over a bridge – the effect was quite spectacular, and within a few minutes everybody was up on their feet and dancing to the music. We repeated that performance three nights running with our Southern sales force on the first night, and the Northerners the second – they were especially riotous! For the third night, Nigel Lawson had asked me if I would do a final show for the local Conservatives, and even they seemed excited by the occasion. I don't think they'd ever experienced anything like it in their lives.

The Merit Awards were given to people who had made an out-standing contribution to the company – whatever their job might be. Every shop would nominate its candidate, and the same went for head office and warehousing staff. Nominations would then be pared down by area managers and so forth until eventually we would be left with perhaps fifty finalists. We'd have a panel of eight judges who were staff council members and who would then select winners from the fifty. When it came to the announcement of the awards, I would be given a sealed envelope containing the names of the winners – I never knew who they were. I'd then announce each name and we'd have a screen behind me which would simultaneously show the prizes; these might include a trip on Concorde or the *QE2*, a week at the Waldorf, two weeks in Mauritius and other incredible holidays. All of our winners more than deserved their awards, and the stories behind some of the nominations were quite amazing. Anne James, who became my secretary, was a winner after she'd broken her leg, had it operated on and returned to work after only three days off with the leg still in plaster.

There was another woman, a fairly junior member of staff in our Lincoln shop, who had suddenly been left all alone to manage the store by a series of illnesses and resignations. Instead of bleating about the unfairness of the situation, for six weeks she got up every morning at 6 a.m. dropped the kids off at school, opened the shop and ran it singlehanded without ever asking for overtime for six weeks. That was the spirit of Next in those days – people were prepared to give a lot without ever counting the cost because we were a hands-on management who gave as much in return.

There's one Merit Award story that I was especially touched by. The winner was the manager of our City store in Edinburgh, and he'd been plagued by ill-luck throughout the course of 1987. In March, his young daughter was rushed into hospital with meningitis and although Stephen Lander was with her every night at hospital, he didn't miss a day's work at his store. Fortunately the child recovered, but very shortly afterwards Stephen himself was taken into hospital with appendicitis. When he returned to work four weeks later he discovered that his shop had fallen behind its targets. By the end of that season he had not only made up the shortfall, but he'd actually exceeded his targets by 10% – and that after all the stress he'd suffered during those previous months. I decided that for once I would show the prizes before announcing the winners. The lights dropped and there was a dramatic silence before three beautiful Ford Escort XR3I Cabriolets were driven on stage. We'd always given away holidays before, so this was especially exciting. Stephen's was the first name to come out of the envelope. I remember the emotion as he walked on stage. I put my arms around Stephen as he said, 'I can't believe this is happening after all that's happened this year . . .' The tears were pouring down his face – and mine. They were great nights.

The first conference we held after the launch of *Next for men* nearly ended in tragedy. We decided to hold the event at the old Talk of the Town in London. We'd always played a few games on stage, much as we had at Pippa Dee. We'd recently introduced catering to Next so we thought it would be both fun and appropriate to have a pastry-making game. Having done my little introductory bit, I handed over to Terry Cook from the Training Department, and took my seat in the audience. Terry started off by telling us she'd like us to meet her 'assistant', at which point Donna Bennett – also from the Training Department – walked up on stage, bearing a tray. She was looking up at the stage lights as she came, and suddenly she disappeared. Everyone laughed, assuming it was part of the act. I realized it wasn't: dazzled by the lights, *Donna had walked straight into a hole in the stage with a 25-foot drop below*. In a cold sweat, I ran round the back and down beneath the stage. There I found Donna – the fall had so taken her by surprise that she'd been completely relaxed as she fell and, incredibly, nothing was broken. 'Have I ruined the show?' she asked me, before we both burst into tears. Someone came with some brandy, which I gratefully drank. 'George, I think that was for me,' said Donna, and of course she was absolutely right!

By now people had realized something was amiss, so Donna and I went back on stage and she was presented with flowers before being taken to hospital. She returned home that night, and the following day I called to find out how she was. The poor girl was practically immobile by then, because her bruised body had stiffened overnight. The day after that Liz and I went round to see her and we arranged for her to be examined by Leicester's top orthopaedic surgeon. When Donna had recovered, we gave her a holiday with her husband. We really did care about people. We would go out of our way to be supportive in times of trouble, because we were genuinely concerned about the welfare of the team.

My management style wasn't of the text-book variety, and often it wasn't to the taste of my peers. When I was fired from Next one of the accusations levelled at me was that I was 'autocratic'. If being 'autocratic' means caring about every part of the business and wanting to remain in touch with it, then yes, I was autocratic. A few months before my firing, in the Autumn of 1988 we were in trouble with the Ethical Society. It was a Friday afternoon and I got a message from Anne, my secretary, that Mike Walters of the *Daily Mail* wanted to speak to me about Next's alleged infringement of the advertising standards regulations. Mike told me that the Ethical Society had released a press report, listing the top 'offenders'. Did I know that Next headed up the list? I did not. This was a serious matter, and because it was quasi-legal, I went straight to John Roberts' office to discover if he knew anything about it. 'What's going on here?' I asked him, and when he expressed ignorance of the affair, I was very angry and went into the attack. 'You're the legal department, aren't you? Surely this is your domain?'

It eventually emerged that there were many inaccuracies in the report which referred to companies not under Next's control at the time. We were therefore able to injunct the report, and save Next's name.

However, such incidents, and the criticism of me in which they resulted, were to come much later, when Next had ceased being the happy and informal compay it had started out as, and had become a vast corporation with systems and structures. In our early years, we may have been unconventional, but there was never any doubt that our unstructured management style was not only avant-grande, but that it worked. In March 1985 recognition came from the *Guardian* who made me their Young Businessman of the Year. The award was presented to me by Dr David Owen at a splendid Mansion House luncheon, and in my acceptance speech I made it clear that as far as I was concerned the award was not for me alone: '[The success of Next] is all down to a team of people, all pulling in the same direction and, probably the most important element, all getting a lot of fun as well as satisfaction.' That was what Next was all about.

I received many warm letters of congratulations from friends, colleagues, shareholders and institutions, many of whom made witty comments about the word 'young'. Nevertheless I was still only 43. Among all the correspondence was a note from Trevor Morgan, whose humorous opening was to prove curiously prophetic. *'Having tried, and failed, to get you on the phone several times recently, I have come to the regretful conclusion that you have been sacked. This is obviously very unfair after being made Young Businessman of the Year, but that's modern business for you, not the leisurely gentlemanly pursuit that it was in my day.'*

The Mini-Departmentals

In October 1984, we had opened our first mini-departmental stores in Edinburgh's Princes Street and Bristol's Broadmead. Both incorporated Next and *Next for men* as well as a shoe department and – for the first time – a café. In Bristol we also included a florist. There were many reasons for expanding Next in this manner, but principle among these was the realization that our best way forward was *organic* growth, as opposed to growth by takeover of other businesses. Our aim was to offer a wider range of goods to the same group of customers. We could have expanded by moving up or downmarket, but our view was that we understood the ABC1 consumer and we were best placed to continue selling to that group of people. Any movement into another socio-economic group would, in any case, dilute our image.

There was a further logic behind the creation of the mini-departmentals, based on economics. If we were going to continue our phenomenal growth (that August, profits had risen from £13.6m in 1983 to £20.6m), we would need more sites and we would therefore have to take on virtually any size of unit that came available. If we were offered a 6,000 square foot site we would be foolish to turn it down, if only because the larger the site, the less you actually pay per square foot – if we could then actually fill that space with merchandise we'd get a very good return. We couldn't then do as Hepworths had done, which was simply fill its large stores with more of the same goods. Our approach would be innovative: the only profitable way of using the space would be to develop a range of different products. As we opened each of the large stores, we might not use all of the space immediately; we would hold it back until we had developed and produced the ranges to fill it. In Bristol, for instance, we kept the top floor closed off, holding it back for the Interiors range we were already planning. This expansion with the new ranges would provide our stores with a 'complete' shopping environment which hitherto they'd lacked. The first of our shops to really achieve this, in my view, was our Regent Street store which included *Next Interiors* for the very first time. Property developers – and, indeed, retailers – set a different value to different parts of any pitch. We recognized that there were 'cheaper' areas of the store, but we knew that we could use those areas to create an attractive atmosphere that would then draw people into our stores. There's a fabulous shopping mall in Dallas which I visited recently, and which illustrates the theory. From the first and second floors of the complex you look down on to a beautiful ice rink in the basement (which is the 'cheap' space). Now, that ice rink probably doesn't take as much money as the rest of the mall, but it gives the whole place a great atmosphere which attracts more customers. That's a creative approach to using 'unusable' space. In Regent Street we took the notion one step further, by breaking the biggest retailing rule of them all: we used 'Zone A' space (the expensive front area) for a coffee bar and flower shop, neither of which are big money spinners and would normally be assigned 'cheap' space. The result was a wonderful sensory experience at the front of the store which drew customers in. Such details have a subliminal effect on the customer, but there is no doubt in my mind that they work. Had we had any doubts, our takings at Regent Street would have dispelled them swiftly.

We chose Edinburgh and Bristol partly because they were towns we'd come to understand, and partly because in both cases we were given the opportunity to buy the pitches at competitive prices. Edinburgh was an unusual challenge: we already had a ladies' wear shop in Princes Street, and the new pitch we bought was two doors away from the original store. The two shops were separated by a branch of Jaeger. Running above these three stores was a large first-floor area which was very cheap, because nobody wanted it. We bought it, thus linking our two sites, and designed the whole so that people were led through the space: in that cheap space upstairs, we had a large men's wear department, shoes and a café overlooking Edinburgh Castle – this last was the bait. We'd flown in the face of convention, but in doing so we drew the customers upstairs and made a lot of money out of that cheap first-floor space.

While the Jenkins group and Tina Ellis had been busy developing the Next men's wear store concept, I'd brought in a young design group called David Davies Associates to redesign the Hepworths' men's wear sites. It was David Davies who would develop our big store concept. I'd been introduced to David back in 1982 by Malcolm Riddell, of Conran Associates, and I remember going to meet him and his interior designer partner, Peter Kent, in the tiny Shoreditch offices they occupied at the time. They were a very young company with no pedigree whatsoever, but I immediately had a good feeling about David and Peter and the way they worked. I often base my decisions about people on a gut reaction, and David Davies Associates were to prove my early instinct right. I have always enjoyed developing close one-to-one relationships with the people with whom I'm working on projects, and the meeting with David was the beginning of one of those periods of great friendship and achievement. After transforming the Hepworth stores at Reading and Romford (his first major design contract), David worked on the mini-department stores in Bristol and Edinburgh before further developing the big store concept with our 'complete' stores in Regent Street, Newcastle, Chester and Exeter. I was very closely involved with all of these projects, because, as with the design of our clothes, I knew what I was trying to achieve, but needed someone with expertise to realize my vision. During that period of development, I moved away from the Next product and became more deeply involved in the design of our stores. It was a wonderfully creative time, and I enjoyed the challenge each of our new stores presented.

A Magical Formula

Another foreign store that had influenced me, and to which I kept returning for inspiration, was Hermès in the Rue de Saint Honoré in Paris. It was a fascinating place to visit, because although it was breaking every possible retailing convention, it was always bustling with activity and quite evidently taking vast amounts of money. The store has a very small door (generally considered a bad thing) leading immediately on to a scarf counter, which is always crowded with Japanese tourists. People love bustle in stores, and that counter combined with the narrow entrance creates an excitement which draws other customers in. In spite of the crowds at the entrance, you can still see a staircase as you walk into that store. Were it not visible, the chances are you might not bother to venture upstairs. But because it is, the incentive to do so is there. What Hermès have achieved, then, is a combination of bustle and enticing vistas. It's a magical formula which we endeavoured to apply as we developed our larger stores.

You've got to make things easy for your customer, and that means leading them around your space in an obvious way. People don't read signs, so what you have to do is lead them quite naturally from one point to the next. Debenhams in Oxford Street is close to getting it right, but when I first visited that store I walked straight past the escalator without seeing it. I bet that their first floor is relatively quiet simply because there's no obvious way of getting up there. As a retailer, it's your job to convert 'bad' space into 'good' space by creating a natural flow which carries your customer right the way round your store. In later years, when I became interested in gardening I realized that these vistas which prompt the flow of customers and which I was trying to create in my stores, were to be found in the great gardens of the world, such as Wisley, Hidcote and Sissinghurst.

I believe that we achieved the right effect in our Chester store which opened in 1984, and incorporated the first of our Next restaurants. The developer had let us have the property relatively cheaply – £140,000 a year for 25,000 square feet – the reason being that the store had a narrow frontage. In conventional terms the wider your frontage, the more 'valuable' the property. What we did was put cosmetics and jewellery right at the front of the store, with ladies' wear at the back. As people came in, they immediately saw a staircase, which was designed in such a way as to encourage them to climb upstairs: it wasn't steep and narrow, and it had two landings on the way up which meant that from the bottom the climb didn't appear too daunting. As I have said, the effect on customers of such design details is subliminal, but very real. Chester was the first of the large stores that I bought. It was a lovely old listed building, formerly a branch of Woolworths, and as we developed our ranges, so we were able to reap the benefits of having all the space at a relatively cheap price. David's design for the store meant that we didn't suffer in the slightest from the narrow frontage, and in fact Chester became one of our most profitable outlets. We'd beaten the property guy at his own game! The Chester store subsequently won The Silver Retail Environment Award 1986 from a body called Design and Art Direction.

I've already spoken about some of the things we did in our Regent Street store, which remains to this day one of my favourites. The way we overcame the store's natural disadvantages continues to give me a great deal of satisfaction. I'd inherited the property from Hepworths for whom it had been the premier site, with an annual turnover of approximately £1.4m. The store was massive, with a large basement which Hepworths weren't using – the ground floor alone was more than adequate for their purposes. When Next moved in, we converted that basement into our men's wear department, and used the large ground floor area for interiors, ladies' wear, shoes, accessories, flowers and the coffee bar. For the first time, we had a store which had that 'complete' environment that I've described. Conventional wisdom dictated that our men's wear would, by necessity, suffer from being relegated to the basement, but in fact that wasn't the case at all. Once more, David Davies' design of the store first of all drew people in off the street – the fresh coffee and flowers did that – and then enticed them down the wide stairs. And although the department couldn't be seen from the street, it actually took more than Hepworths had done when they had occupied the whole of the ground floor. We moved turnover from Hepworths £1.4m to a handsome £5m – all the proof we needed that our innovative approach was right.

New Offices at Enderby

David Davies and Brian Johnson – one of his partners, and a talented three-dimensional designer – were also highly influential in the design of our new head offices at Enderby which came second to Richard Rogers's Lloyds building in the 1987 *Financial Times'* Architecture at Work Award. The building had to be very special, for I wanted it to symbolize the Next corporate culture. Somehow it would have to link up to the old Van Allen building, so that the people who remained behind in the old structure would still feel part of the new one. This was everybody's Head Office and it was important that no one should feel left out. With these thoughts in mind, I approached four different architects, all of whom came up to Enderby to make their presentations. Their ideas weren't bad, but they were all pretty similar and none grabbed us as being the right one.

We were very disheartened, and decided that there was no way we were going to get what we wanted if we left the design of our offices to somebody else. Brian Johnson therefore went away and found a small architectural practice called ORMS (Oliver Richards, Martin Sherley), with whom we would develop a suitable plan; once again, I had returned to my old method of having a very strong idea and putting it across to experts who would then convert it into a product. Having worked very closely with me in the past, Brian and David were a vital link in this process: we developed the concept together and it was then carried through by the architects. The building that emerged was everything I had hoped for: it reflected the Next culture and was charged with an amazing energy which people would pick up on the minute they walked into the reception. Our old offices were linked to the new by a mall of Next shops where we would test out our display ideas and new ranges – a throwback, perhaps, to that original mock shop in the Kendalls building which had so impressed the *Vogue* ladies. Inside, the new building offered a wonderful sense of space, with views from the ground floor right up to the buying floor at the top, thirty feet above. Everywhere you went, you could see the activity on all the different floors – it was quite an amazing place. My office was on the first floor, at the hub of all this activity, with a door that was always open.

The Next headquarters was the last project David Davies would work on with me. Apart from the big stores, David updated our ladies' wear stores, and worked on Next Essentials, the hairdressing concept, cosmetics and Interiors. Our working relationship had been a very special one, but by mid-1986 we'd reached a point where I felt Next needed to move on. David's business had expanded from the intimacy of the small consultancy into a factory. I'd always felt that a large design group wasn't right for Next, because it precluded the level of involvement that we always required to achieve the best result. To be fair on David, I had also distanced myself by that time from the design part of the business. I had become very preoccupied with corporate matters and especially the imminent purchase of Grattans. In the end a parting of the ways was inevitable. Happily, David and I are still very close.

Next Interiors

The opening of the Regent Street store in August 1985 heralded the arrival of Next Interiors. Liz and I had felt that home furnishings was a direction we should be moving in, and we'd been impressed by what we'd seen at Tricia Guild's Designer's Guild on the King's Road. We thought that if we could get in somebody like Tricia to develop our range, we'd be able to get the concept off the ground more quickly, and without all the pain of developing a new range from scratch. It really did seem the best idea at the time, and we duly had our first meeting with

Tricia.

The deal we struck with Tricia gave her a five-year contract and a percentage of all sales of her designs. I think Tricia was as excited as we were by the prospect of Next Interiors, and happy with the idea of developing the new product alongside Sandy Dobson – who was in charge of the Next Interiors project – Liz, myself and David Davies who was still, at that time, closely involved with Next. Unlike the rest of our operation, Next Interiors would be run from a London office, and for this purpose we bought a house just off the King's Road, in Oakley Street, which also served as a showhouse where we could take our own photographs and bring the press.

We launched with four ranges – Checkers, Neapolitan, Flowers and Shadows – with the aim that they would appeal to varying levels of taste. The product range was wide too, offering a complete selection of goods for the home – furniture, wallpaper, bedlinens and even drawer liners, air fresheners and lighting. We also produced a Next Interiors catalogue, which was not only a way of presenting the range but also gave customers the possibility of buying through mail order. It was the first step along the road to the Next Directory. The launch of Interiors went well, but we soon realized that it wasn't going to take off as quickly as our fashion ranges. We found that there was a distinct North-South divide, and that while our shops in Kingston and Regent Street were doing tremendous business (£8,000 and £20,000+ a week respectively), Hull was taking a worrying £800. The reason for this discrepancy lay, I believe, in the fact that trends in interior design are not as obviously conspicuous as trends in fashion. You only have to walk on to the street to see what people are wearing and what the current look is, but it's less easy to gain access to those people's homes and discover how they have dressed their house – the influences are therefore less powerful. Northern taste hadn't caught up with London, but I knew that given time, we would make the concept work across the country. Over the following three years, sales in the north did indeed begin to take off.

In the meantime, however, there was much work to be done. We had to react as we had always reacted at Next: we travelled to the various towns where we were having problems and went out into the community, talking to people – it's the only way of finding out their needs and what it is they want to buy. Perhaps that's where our conflicts with Tricia began. A divide began to form between her and the team at Next who felt that although she was reaping rich rewards from the concept, she wasn't prepared to put in the necessary leg work to get it right. The signs of trouble had been there from before the launch, in fact, and I remember that the Wednesday night before we opened Regent Street, we were to have a launch party in the store. I popped in just before the event only to discover that everyone was in tears. Apparently Tricia had been in and played hell with the team for not getting the flowers right. Those girls had worked through the night and to me the store looked wonderful.

The incident brought into focus our basic problem with Tricia – she wasn't part of the Next culture. Personally I always related very well to her, and the team she headed up produced an excellent range for us. She is, however, a very strong-minded individual who is used to running her own show, and she simply wasn't able to adapt to the larger environment of Next. Next people didn't draw lines between the different parts of the business. They worked for the total good of the company. Whereas a specialist outsider – like Tricia – inevitably concentrated on her own part of the business. This basic difference in approach meant that she would never fit in with us. Gradually her involvement with Next was scaled down. She produced a second range, but after eighteen months we moved the operation up to Enderby (where it should have been from the outset) and took control of it ourselves under Colin Shiner. With the benefit of hindsight I can see now that we would have been better off developing the Interiors concept from within the organization from the beginning – I have always said that I prefer to start with a blank piece of paper, and I should have stuck by that belief.

Our venture into hairdressing in March 1986 would prove this point. The idea came to me after we'd worked on a cosmetics range with Molton Brown. I knew absolutely nothing about hairdressing, so I decided to get Molton Brown to develop the concept for me and presently we opened a hairdressing school in the Wella Training Rooms in the Marylebone Road. Our first salon was in the Newcastle store and, to be frank, it has never really taken off. I should have known that in order to get a business going you have to inject your own personality into it for many months and – in our case – the personality of Next. We couldn't merely buy a formula off the shelf. But these are lessons you learn along the way. I can see now that whenever I relied on somebody from outside Next, the early stages were always good, but once the concept was up and running problems would start to surface. In the light of experience, I am far more aware and a little more cautious now about entering into any similar relationships.

Expanding at home and abroad

We were always looking for new ways to expand, and in the Spring of 1983 I'd had my first foray into foreign stores, with disappointing results. We'd had many letters from abroad with suggestions and requests that we open stores in this town or that. Terence Conran had given me an introduction to a colleague who was responsible for Mothercare's foreign expansion, and I remember going to meet him in London. He warned me of the pitfalls of going abroad. Notwithstanding, I decided that we should have a trial run and Jeremy Dexter, from our property department, duly sought out some appropriate sites in Germany, eventually acquiring four in Wiesbaden, Frankfurt, Essen and Aachen. The initial launches were wonderful, but gradually the stores began to perform less and less well, and after about eighteen months we'd taken the decision to close them down. I can see now where we went wrong: fashion is an emotional product, and if you are going to tap into the emotions of your customer, you have to immerse yourself in their society, live and breathe their culture before you launch your product on the market. Every country's fashion development is different from that of its neighbours. In Germany, women have a more ostentatious attitude than here; they will gladly pay an extra £100 to have a jumper elaborately embroidered, for instance. British women, on the other hand, prefer a cleaner line and a more understated look. So you can't simply say that a range that sells well in England will necessarily sell well in Germany. Getting the look even marginally wrong can mean the difference between profit and loss, so you have to make adaptations which are based on your intimate knowledge of the new market. We lacked that knowledge and although our merchandise was broadly right, we had failed to recognize and incorporate those subtle – but essential – differences. Our experience in Germany is a lesson for any fashion retailer looking forward to 1992 and the European market: if you want to sell in volume, you have to study your market very carefully before you enter it, and adapt to its needs accordingly.

Our movement from the small store into the mini-department and 'complete' stores between 1984 and 1986 had by no means resolved the problem of our pressing need for more space. As we planned Interiors, we scouted around for sites that would enable us to continue expanding on the High Street. In the summer of 1985 Jeremy Dexter heard that the troubled Raybeck group was selling off its loss-making Lord John and Werff clothing stores, and that chairman Ben Raymond had all but signed a deal with Stephen Marks of French Connection. There was some discussion about price and, seeing an opportunity, we stepped in and bought the 142 shops for £11.5m, which was an excellent price. I recall Stephen Marks phoning me saying we'd paid too much!

This was our first major takeover and inevitably it had an impact on the way we worked. We had acquired a large business which we now had to run, and the only solution was to take key people from other parts of the company and transfer them to the new concern. You could argue that the growth pattern we had set ourselves (and with which the City was pressurizing us to continue) would ultimately stretch our management to breaking point and, in fact, one of the criticisms of me when I was fired was that I had built a company which lacked management depth. Of course there was a measure of management dilution as we grew, and of course there were many senior people at Next who were stretched to the limits – I knew that only too well. We responded in the only way we could by training our younger managers into more responsible positions and to this end, we developed a series of training schemes. Our graduate course was always heavily subscribed, and was also open to non-graduates who had some experience at work. Then there was our 'Fast Trackers' scheme, which brought in and trained more senior individuals whose background was other than retailing – the last recruit to this that I remember was a lawyer. Finally, we created a Junior Development Programme, for which we won a national training award. This scheme was for school leavers, and the programme included on-site training in a store, as well as time at one of our five regional training centres. By the time I left Next, some of our young managers were beginning to fill the gaps in our management structure. I knew it would take time, but for a company that was burgeoning like Next there was no alternative.

My role at Next also changed as we expanded. I became increasingly involved in the development of the company, and in satisfying the requirements of the City who not only wanted us to continue increasing our profits, but also demanded a constant flow of information from me – all of which took up my time. With my appointment as Chief Executive of the Hepworth group in January 1985, I moved further away from my early close involvement with our product and its development and into a role that was more and more corporate, and less and less to my liking.

8

NEXT plc

Joe Hepworth

In January 1986 everything began to change. Our expansion made it imperative for me to appoint some senior people to administer to the company's corporate needs. I therefore promoted John Roberts – the lawyer – to the position of Group Corporate Director. Little did I realize that it was a move that would have a deep effect on Liz's and my future. I also brought on to the Board as Finance Director a very able fellow called Robert Cooper, a merchant banker whom I'd met a few months previously.

On the 3rd of the month there was another significant change. We took the step of dropping the group name of J. Hepworth and Son, and replacing it with the by now more appropriate Next plc. Although the Hepworth family had long since relinquished any active involvement in the company, they were still substantial shareholders, and I had thought it only proper to consult the senior family member – Joe Hepworth – about our proposed change of name. We duly met for lunch at Coutts, where Joe gave our decision his blessing – he was touched that we should have taken the trouble to solicit his opinion, and could see that it made sense to incorporate the group's activities under the banner of Next plc.

It was my second meeting with Joe, whom I'd only met for the first time six months previously, when he and his wife had invited Liz and me to their fortieth wedding anniversary celebration at the Carlton Tower hotel. What an occasion that was! The invitation had followed a very nice letter from Joe, thanking us for all we'd done for J. Hepworth and Son, as it was at the time, and suggesting we join the family for a 'small dinner one evening'. When we arrived at the hotel we were directed up to the first floor. As we climbed the stairs we saw scores of elegant people milling around in ballgowns and dinner jackets. Still looking for my 'small dinner party', I asked a hotel staff member where I might find my host, and he indicated a room across the corridor, adding that Mr Hepworth was the small man with one arm. I poked my head around the door, only to see before me some 300 guests! So much for the intimate family get-together! Joe and his wife were absolutely charming and gave us the honour of seating us at their top table for the dinner. It was a riotous affair, especially when Joe stood up to make his speech which included many a ribald joke about his assembled relatives – they were a very fun-loving family. Towards the end, he said, 'Can all the family stand up, please, as I'd like to thank the man who's paid for tonight. Let's have a round of applause for George Davies!' I was greatly moved by the gesture, and remember that evening with affection.

Joe Hepworth and I remained in friendly contact over the years to follow, although our relationship was put under some stress when his son (also Joe), who had a wine bar in Lavender Hill, offered to help us run our restaurant operation. It didn't work out so we parted company. In spite of this, I was surprised and saddened not to hear anything from Joe senior when Liz and I were fired from Next. I can only assume that he held me responsible for losing him a lot of money. Like the City, he had perhaps forgotten how much more I had made him over the years . . .

In the January of 1986, however, the City was still on my side, but they were putting me under tremendous pressure to continue the pace of growth. With hindsight I now believe that I should have reacted to the challenge differently. Rather than constantly coming up with new ideas, I should have consolidated the concepts we had established already. The City might not have liked it, for our profits certainly wouldn't have risen as steeply, but I might still be at Next today. But that's all speculation, and at the time there appeared to be no alternative to the innovative path we chose to follow.

Accessories, Shoes, Lingerie and Jewellery

The birth of the 'complete' store had prompted us to develop new ranges. But there was another important factor – we were acquiring scores of smaller sites as well. If we simply stocked these with more ladies' and men's wear, we would kill off the exclusivity of Next, and we therefore had to find new ways of filling the space. And that meant more ranges, aimed at the same group of customers. In August 1986 we launched the first of our Accessory Shops and Shoe Shops, and a month later, Next Lingerie came on to the High Street in forty-two shops. Cosmetics was the next concept, which we developed with Molton Brown.

Jewellery was another concept that pleased me enormously, and which we launched with the opening of the High Street Kensington store in May 1987. Having visited a number of jewellery stores I had begun to get the feeling that while chains like Ratners were offering jewellery at cheap prices, the ranges were very downmarket. At the other end of the scale I greatly admired fashion jewellery retailers like Butler and Wilson but they weren't accessible to the average shopper and in any case had no presence in the provinces. It was the same old story: there was a gap in the middle of the market which we could fill. We were very fortunate in that Beverley Holtom, who we brought in to develop the range for us, was highly talented and, having worked as a designer/buyer for Butler and Wilson, she was attuned to the taste levels of the more discerning customer. We decided that we would have two ranges. The first was the non-precious fashion jewellery, which took off immediately and has remained a strong product. The second was precious jewellery. The idea here was that we would provide, along with the precious items, a consultative, advisory service. This was much slower in taking off. It was still less successful than the costume jewellery when I left, needing time and talent to project the concept. Apart from the jewellery, we also introduced masculine products such as cufflinks, tie pins, watches and so forth, all of which complemented the image we had created in *Next for men*.

Children's wear, like jewellery, was launched at High Street Kensington, four months after the opening of the store. It was part of our strategy to turn these larger stores into places for the whole family, and kids' wear remains to this day one of the most successful parts of our retailing business. Bob Williams, who had worked on children's wear with me back in the Littlewoods days, moved over from men's wear and headed up the development of our children's range, together with Wendy Richardson, another founding member of the Next team.

The other important step we took in the August of 1986, as we expanded into new ranges, was to split ladies' wear into Next Too and Collection. The logic behind the move was that ladies' wear was becoming over-exposed on the High Street and that there was a danger of women ceasing to come to us for fear of finding themselves dressed in the same outfits as all their friends and colleagues. Our philosophy had always been to keep our ranges tightly edited – as I've written elsewhere, too much choice in a store is confusing – so we couldn't counteract the problem by simply giving a wider selection of garments. No, the only solution was to divide ladies' wear into two parts. At the outset we simply refitted some of our shops to create a slightly different look for Next Too, and then developed two separate ranges which were aimed at broadly the same customer. Soon, however, we felt we should define more closely the Next Too customer, and that was when we began to go astray. We'd always believed in developing the raw talent and energy of young people, and we decided to bring in top young graduates from the Royal College of Art to develop a younger, more contemporary look for Next Too. The trouble with these people was that although they were undoubtedly talented as designers, they didn't understand retailing and Next Too began to go seriously offbeat. Some of the ranges were successful, but there was no consistency, and in mid 1988 we decided to merge Too and Collection into a single range. By then, in any case, we had launched Next Originals (January 1988) which reflected the ladies' wear concept we'd started with back in 1982.

With all this development into new ranges we began to consider a further major purchase, and shortly after completing the Raybeck deal, which had given me the Lord John shops in September 1985, I entered into discussions with the board of House of Fraser. It was through Robert Cooper, one of the Directors of Next's merchant bankers, Kleinwort Benson, that I began to investigate the possibility of buying part of the House of Fraser group. Robert was a very able man – I later recruited him as Group Finance Director in January 1986 – and he suggested to me that the Al-Fayed brothers might have bought the House of Fraser simply because they wanted Harrods, and that they might wish to dispose of the rest of the group. Just before the Christmas of 1985 I met Ali and Mohammed Al-Fayed and our discussions progressed to the stage where we were talking about a £450m deal to purchase all of the House of Fraser stores bar Harrods. However, we never got beyond that point, largely I suspect because Tiny Rowland had launched his attack on the Al-Fayeds and there was pressure on them to hold on to the whole group. In any case the deal faded away. I've always had a close connection with Ali, and after the sacking from Next I looked at the House of Fraser stores for him. I'm full of admiration for the way in which he has tackled the difficult job of running the group, without being distracted by the intense pressure he has recently been under.

Buying new sites and producing new ranges was the obvious way of meeting the ever more ambitious targets Next was being set by the City (in the August of 1986 we would announce profits of £27.7m, which gave rise to a prediction of £40 million for the following year – we actually made £42.3m). But pitching my vision into the future, I could see that this method of keeping up our rate of growth would soon be curtailed by prohibitive High Street rents – pressure on retailing space would only serve to push those rents up, and eventually our property commitments would make it very difficult for us to make money. And even if we were to continue buying High Street property, there would come a time when we would simply run out of places to buy. There had to be another way forward.

Back to Mail Order

It was at this point that I began to think about mail order, an industry I had learned about all those years ago at Littlewoods and then School Care. I soon realized that nothing much had changed since those times, that mail order was still perceived by the public as the downmarket alternative to High Street retailing, and that nobody had tried to bring it upmarket and into the 1980s. Mail order had been founded on what was called the four Cs: *commission* (because there were agents who looked after the customers in different areas, and who were paid by commission); *convenience* (because in days gone by shops were either too far away or they didn't stock the goods); *comprehensive* offer (because you had, in effect, a whole department store in a book); and *credit* (because that was how payment of the goods was arranged). By the 1980s the mail order industry was still holding to these principles which were quite obviously out of date. The comprehensiveness was still there and an element of convenience. But most catalogues still had a twenty-eight-day delivery date, which was no longer acceptable to a faster-moving society; the credit advantages had been eroded by the availability of many alternative sources of credit; and the agent method of selling had long since passed out of common practice. So just like Hepworths when I first joined it, mail order was being ignored by many of its potential customers, for no reason other than that the industry had failed to bring itself in line with the changing times. I was convinced that if we could only adapt mail order to the needs of the 1980s' customer – and, more specifically, the Next customer – we would be able to continue our expansion without having to rely on expensive High Street property.

There were other influences at work, which over the months had turned me against the High Street and made me think 'mail order'. City centres appeared to be becoming increasingly violent. The High Street was no longer the sort of place where families and people over 30 enjoyed spending their time. At Next we'd experienced problems at first hand with a particularly nasty robbery at our South Molton Street branch. Eight youths had marched in and cleared the place out. Our staff were amazing, resisting and pursuing the criminals as best they could, but in the end there was very little they could do. We'd also had an incident at our Wolverhampton branch where a man had tried to buy goods with an allegedly stolen Barclaycard. When the police tried to arrest him, a fight broke out, in the course of which the man was sadly killed, which everyone deeply regretted. For the following days there were riots outside Next which resulted in the shop having to be closed down for a while; worse than that, some of our staff received letters in which their lives were threatened. It was a bad time.

Grattans

I first met Roger Seelig in the Summer of 1983. He was Corporate Finance Director (mergers and takeovers) at Morgan Grenfell, and it was he who had made the presentation to the Hepworths Board when Terence Conran put in his proposal to us. Over the years our paths had crossed on several occasions, and we'd been brought together again in early 1986 by Underwoods, on whose Board we both served as non-executive directors. As I looked at possible ways of developing Next, I would discuss my ideas with Roger, and from time to time he would suggest deals that he thought might suit us. It was during one of these discussions, when I had mentioned to Roger my thoughts about mail order, that he said to me, 'You ought to meet David Jones at Grattan's. Roger acted for Grattans and he knew that they might be interested in doing a deal with Next. I knew that Grattans were one of our foremost mail order companies, renowned for their excellent systems, but that they'd been through a difficult patch in recent years. If we could link up with them, we would be able to move into mail order in a matter of months. I told Roger straight away that if David Jones was interested in talking to us, then I'd like to meet him.

At our initial meeting, which took place in London at the beginning of June 1986, David and I hit it off straight away. Here was a man who understood mail order and who spoke about the subject in a way that impressed me – he'd been in the business since joining Kays of Worcester at the age of 17, coming in as a clerk and leaving as Managing Director of a subsidiary of GUS (Great Universal Stores). As Grattans' Deputy Chairman and Managing Director it was he who had turned the company's pre-tax loss of £1.1 million in 1983, to profits of

£16m in 1985/6. The more we spoke, the more I could see the logic of bringing together the strengths of Grattans with those of Next. While we had the merchandising expertise, they had the systems – Grattans had pioneered sophisticated computer systems which allowed them to process orders more efficiently. But most importantly of all, David shared my vision of what we could achieve together.

We met again the following day and came to the conclusion that we should bring our two companies together. Although our usual merchant bankers were Kleinwort Benson, on this occasion I wanted Roger Seelig and Morgan Grenfell to represent Next's interests; they were, in fact, the bank that usually advised Grattans, so David chose Ansbacher in their stead and the negotiating began. From the outset this was to be a friendly bid, and although Next was effectively taking over Grattans we always referred to it as a merger. That is a decision I have often reflected on. My enthusiasm for the Grattans deal led me to bend over backwards in my efforts to maintain the atmosphere of friendship and cooperation that had characterized the birth of this deal. After all, I trusted David Jones and thought him to be as excited as I was about the Next-Grattans union – I still think so. One of the provisos the Grattans Board set, and to which I agreed, was that I should delay my promotion to Chairman and Chief Executive of Next until October 1987 and that Mike Stoddart – our current Chairman – should remain *in situ* for that time. There were many other issues on which Next acceded, not because we had to in every case, but because we saw our so-called merger with Grattans as a marriage of two complementary businesses.

On 30 June 1986 Next launched a £299m agreed bid for Grattans and their shares shot up from 404p to 530p. Brokers' circulars, quoted in the national press, declared that the deal was, '. . . the only retail deal to date with visible and obvious synergy. It creates a unique group with numerous routes to growth in the future.' Everyone could see the logic behind uniting Next style with Grattans' mail order technology, to launch a new type of catalogue that would be marketed under the Next name. For my part, I believed that without Grattans, Next simply couldn't create and launch that which would become the Next Directory. Moreover, I was excited by the prospect of working with David

112

Jones, who would become Deputy Managing Director of Next. Whenever I have embarked on a new project that's fired me, the enthusiasm has always been generated very largely by the people involved. In David's case, I felt that we'd found someone who was not only strong, but who actually had disciplines that complemented my own. He didn't have any pretensions to being creative or to being a product developer, but he did understand mail order systems which was an area I was weaker on. There was nothing in our relationship at that stage that would suggest that our dealings with one another would ever be anything other than friendly. In a *Sunday Times* article following the 'merger', David was quoted as saying, 'Jones and Davies are not going to fall out.'

With the Grattans purchase we entered into an ever more busy period. Everyone was working flat out at Enderby and at Bradford, the Grattans' headquarters, none more than the senior members of my merchandise team who would be responsible for creating the product for our new mail order initiative, planned for launch in 1988. Naturally, we had teething troubles, but no more than you would expect when you have two teams coming from differing points of view. I always believed that was the strength of the relationship but not all my team – Liz, Frances Mossman, and the like – always agreed with me.

My time was also taken up with the conceiving, planning and launching of all the new ranges. The Grattans purchase had perhaps diverted me from the search for an appropriate High Street retailing chain to buy, and since the collapse of my discussions with the House of Fraser, I had had no significant talks with anybody else. In the Spring of 1987, however, a new opportunity suddenly appeared on the horizon.

Combined English Stores and Ratners

Murray Gordon, the Chairman of Combined English Stores, was somebody I'd been in touch with over the months. He'd told me that he was under pressure from Gerald Ratner, the jeweller, who wanted to buy CES. It wasn't difficult to see why: the group – which comprised Salisburys, Zales, Collingwoods/Weirs and Paige, as well as camping and travel interests and the German ladies' wear chain Biba – would provide its purchaser with 870 prime retail sites. Murray had told me that his business was in good shape, and that he didn't want a Ratners takeover, but he'd hinted that if he were to sell, he'd like Next to put in a bid. I said that we would be interested if the price was right. I was very surprised, therefore, to hear one day in May that a deal between Ratner and CES was about to be completed. I remember the news coming through late one evening while I was round at the office of Lynne Franks', the fashion PR we'd appointed to handle the Directory. I got on the phone straight away, and eventually traced Murray at his merchant bank, Samuel Montagu. 'What the hell's going on?' I asked him. 'I said we would buy you if the deal was right – so why are you going ahead with Ratner without even consulting us?' Murray gave me a vague reply to the effect that Gerald Ratner had been putting him under tremendous pressure. I cut in with the suggestion that he hold the deal back for a few hours so that I could have time to get my Board together: 'Look, I can't tell you over the phone that yes, we'll definitely buy you, but just put Ratner off so that I can call my Board and advisers together tomorrow at 9 a.m.; we'll discuss this and get back to you.' Murray agreed.

At 8.30 a.m. the following day, which I believe was a Friday, Gerald Ratner announced that he had done his deal with CES. Undeterred, I went round to Salomon Brothers, the American bank, whom I'd contacted when Murray and I had first discussed the possibility of doing a deal together. They'd only recently come over to London and felt they lacked the necessary experience in mergers and acquisitions. Roger Seelig suggested I contact Lord Garmoyle and Derek Higgs of Warburg Asset Management. They were keen to do the job, but one of their major clients was Burtons, and they had to clear it with Sir Ralph Halpern. Because it was a Bank Holiday weekend, they were unable to contact Ralph, and we therefore went to Roger's second suggestion, which was Lazards. They joined me with my Board when we met for our 'war council' in Enderby that Bank Holiday Monday. We worked through the figures to see if we could improve on the Ratners' bid, and we then looked at our development strategy in the event of a successful bid. The figures looked good, and the more we looked at our strategy for the future and our increasing hunger for retailing space, the more we felt that here was a deal that we couldn't afford to miss. At one point, several hours into our discussions, I left the room and made a call to Roger Seelig – on this occasion, he wasn't acting for us in any official capacity, but I got along with him well and respected his opinion. His advice to me was that we should try and get hold of the 17% stake that Warburgs had in Combined English Stores – that would clinch the deal.

I returned to the meeting in the Boardroom and told my colleagues about my conversation with Roger and the advisers. Some of the advisers who knew Roger well particularly after the Guinness affair in which Roger was involved, were highly sceptical about his suggestion, saying that there was no logical reason why the bank should sell off its shares in CES at this stage of the proceedings; if they sold now, they argued, they would get a price based on Next's bid, and in the event of somebody coming in with a higher bid, they would lose out. I felt that there was a chance, however, because these deals take weeks and even months to complete, and I argued that those were weeks and months in which the cash from sale of the shares could be earning interest. That night I dined late with John Roberts and at about 11 p.m. I contacted Carol Galley of Warburgs, whom I knew well, and suggested to her the possibility of Warburgs selling us their shares. She didn't dismiss the idea right away, and agreed to discuss it with her boss the next day.

The following morning at 7 a.m., I called Murray Gordon and told him of my progress. I then flew down to London and met him privately at Salomons where I told him that I wasn't at all happy with the way he'd backtracked on our agreement the previous week, but that I was now going to put in a bid for CES and that I expected him to recommend it – even though he'd already recommended the Ratners bid. Murray said that he would go with Next. I then went over to Warburgs where I had a meeting with Carol Galley and another Director called Stephen Zimmerman, and they agreed to sell me their stake in CES. That afternoon I flew back to Enderby and told Michael Stoddart that the way was now clear for our bid, and that with the Warburg shares we now had a terrific head start in the race to acquire Combined English Stores.

In fact it wasn't going to be as easy as I thought. We got a message from the CES bankers – Samuel Montagu – that night that Murray wasn't actually able to recommend our bid. Because he'd already signed irrevocable guarantees with Ratners, if he were to backtrack, Gerald Ratner could sue him for millions of pounds. This time we really felt that we'd reached an impasse. Where could we go from here? After all our efforts, were we going to be blocked at this late stage? None of us could see a solution. Then an idea suddenly came to me: we could go ahead with the bid, without Murray's recommendation. If he then recommended us half an hour later, nobody would be able to accuse him of actively seeking out another buyer. It was a loophole, but that was all we needed. Murray and I met at Salomon's the following morning at 7.45 and we closed the deal. Next had won control of Combined English Stores for £340m. The twist to the tale was that it was CES who had originally sold Kendalls to Hepworths back in 1981, and who had therefore played an indirect part in the creation of Next.

Even though we were locked in battle when we first met, I grew to like and respect Gerald Ratner. Many people have said that they don't warm to him, and perhaps that's because he never reveals very much of himself. He's taken the view that at a time when many people were trying to move upmarket, he would go downmarket. Gerald is a shrewd man and has done extremely well – I hope he continues to do so. In a sense, he created the CES opportunity for me, by forcing the sale with his own bid. Although on that occasion he failed to win CES, he later acquired part of the group from us; Next sold Salisburys and Zales to Ratner in October 1988. Sometimes I can't help feeling that everything in business just goes round in circles! Over the years we've seen each other on and off – one of the most enjoyable occasions was when we both appeared with Sophie Mirman and David Sieff on the Terry Wogan show in November 1988. The programme was abour retailing, and they filmed it from the Littlewoods store on Oxford Street where Terry Wogan was switching on the Christmas lights.

During the months prior to Grattans, and leading up to the CES deal, there had been a tremendous amount of takeover activity – Burtons had bought Debenhams for £560m, while Habitat Mothercare had merged with British Homestores in a £1.5 billion deal. At the time that Grattans and Next got together, I was described in the *Observer* as being 'poised to join the lemming-like rush into high street space', and referring to the abortive talks with the House of Fraser, they said I had been 'straining at the leash to make such a quantum leap for some time'. The description wasn't wholly inaccurate, for I was indeed anxious to acquire the space that would accommodate Next's widening range of businesses. CES had given me some prime city centre sites, but I was now interested in acquiring a stake in suburbia. In the back of my mind I could see that small suburban sites would serve perfectly as pick-up and drop-off points for our developing interests in home shopping. It was Michael Stoddart, our Chairman at the time, who told the Board that Dillons the newsagents had approached Next with the proposal of a management buy-out. The chain of 270 mainly suburban sites was what we'd been looking for, and in July 1987 we bought Dillons for £28.5m.

In April 1988 we increased our stake in suburbia with the £21m purchase of Alfred Preedy and Sons, the 140-strong West Midlands chain of confectioners and newsagents. I think the City found this purchase and the Dillons deal hard to comprehend – how could a chain of suburban newsagents fit into a high class fashion retailing outfit? They couldn't see that I was looking ahead into the future and trying to develop Next's portfolio so that when that future came, we would be able to react to our customers' demands.

In September 1987, after the CES and Dillons purchases, we took out a £100 million convertible Eurobond issue, as a way of refinancing the debt we had incurred by our takeover activity. There were many new ways of borrowing money becoming available at that time, but this seemed the cheapest. It involved issuing a bond to European investors, who would then have the right to convert that bond into shares once the share price had climbed beyond a given point. All this seemed perfectly reasonable in September while our shares were strong and climbing. But just a month later, the stock market Crash brought our share price tumbling down from 360p to 250p, saddling us with a longstanding debt which would have repercussions on our standing in the City.

The Death of My Father

The CES takeover came during one of the busiest and most stressful months of my life, coinciding as it did with the opening both of our new head offices and the High Street Kensington store, as well as the death of my father. I've always rung my mother two or three times a week, and it was when I called her one day during the course of the CES saga that she told me that Dad had a pain in his stomach, but that I wasn't to worry because he was going to see a doctor. The day we closed the CES deal with Murray Gordon, I rang home again as I drove back to Leicester from London. This time I was alarmed by what my mother had to say: 'Your father's in a dreadful way – he can't sleep for the pain.' The following morning I phoned once more, and learned that my father had again been unable to sleep, and that he'd been vomiting through the night. The family doctor was away on a golfing trip, and in any case I was now concerned that my father needed more than a GP. I therefore rang a brilliant gastro-enterologist, David Carr-Locke, whom I'd met six months previously.

David and I had become close friends, and he agreed to see my father straight away. Dad, who was now in terrible pain, was picked up by one of our drivers and driven to the Fielding Johnson Clinic in Leicester. David diagnosed my father's condition right away: he had gall stones, and would need an operation. It was a great relief for us to know at last what was wrong, and that there was a cure. But our relief was to be short-lived, for after operating on Dad the next Monday, David had to tell us that my father had cancer of the pancreas and had between three and twelve months to live. Had Dad been younger (he was now in his seventies), there might have been a further operation to remove the cancer, but at his age there was a likelihood that he wouldn't pull through the surgery. We had to accept that we were going to lose him very soon.

Three days later Liz and I took my parents back to Foston in Leicestershire where we lived. Dad seemed fine, and shortly he returned with my mother to their home in Formby. But within a week, my mother phoned me to say that my father had suffered a relapse and was in agony. I hired a private ambulance, and this time Dad was taken to the Leicester Royal Infirmary. On the Bank Holiday Monday – 25 May – Margaret Thatcher came to Enderby to open the new Next building. We'd hoped my father would be able to make the occasion, but his relapse now made that impossible, and my mother left his bedside very briefly to attend on her own. After the opening ceremony, I remember spying my mother on her own, trying to slip away unnoticed so that she could get back to the hospital. I took Mrs Thatcher over to her and explained that my father was desperately ill. She was absolutely wonderful with my mother and actually wrote a personal note to my father.

As soon as Mrs Thatcher had gone, we all rushed over to the Infirmary where we were met by David Carr-Locke: 'He's going, I'm afraid,' he told us. Liz and I made our way to my father's room, and sat by his bedside with my mother, quietly waiting for the final moment. After about two hours my father suddenly regained consciousness, opened his eyes and asked us how we were all doing. He didn't die that night.

Our High Street Kensington store was opening that week, on Friday 29 May, and on Thursday we had a big press evening. I remember that Bruce Oldfield, the designer, was throwing a party that evening to which Liz and I were invited, but my father's condition was such that we drove back to Leicester as soon as we were able. I'd phoned the hospital from the store and had been told that this time my father really was dying. We sat by his bedside throughout the night, but once more, showing himself the fighter that he was, he lived to see the following day. Dad died two days later, on the Saturday. That morning I sat on his bed and he told me he wasn't going to give up his fight. But, in the end, the enemy proved stronger. I had become closer to my father than ever before during those weeks, and his death left me with a terrible sense of loss. I knew, however, that I had to remain strong for my mother's sake and that my first responsibility was to help her come to terms with her grief. I might have had a day off – I don't really remember – but I felt that the best way for me to cope was to carry on with my work and keep my own grief to myself.

In one way, you can compare it with my sacking from Next. My attitude wasn't to let the pain get the better of me. In both cases, I got up and carried on. Some people react to loss in a different way, and would perhaps accuse me of callousness, but those who were close to me at the time of my father's death – Liz in particular – knew just how much I suffered. That time remains the saddest in my life.

During those weeks of my father's illness I came into frequent contact with David Carr-Locke. He'd originally been recommended to me the April of that year by Keith Dickson, our company doctor, when I was suffering from stomach pains which were very possibly stress-related, but which in any case never proved to be serious. After a brief examination at his surgery, David suggested I come to see him at the Fielding Johnson Hospital, where he could give me a more thorough examination. What he meant was that he could look right inside me by means of an endoscope – I remember realizing that I was going to like David when he put the endoscope down my throat and another up my back passage, and then invited me to have a look myself, with the words, 'Do you feel like being introspective?'!

David is a delightful fellow, one of the most highly respected consultant physicians in gastro-enterology in the country, and a pioneer in the use of endoscopes. My father's death cemented our friendship, and as I learned more about David's work, I became increasingly aware of many of the frustrations of doctors working in the Health Service; although David had some private patients, most of his work was with NHS patients. I believe that big businesses have community responsibilities, and it seemed right to me that Next should in some way support the Leicester Royal Infirmary, and David Carr-Locke's important work. The specific project we became involved in was the development of more sophisticated endoscopes, and Next agreed to fund 50% of the project. I felt it was important that the Health Authority raise the further 50%, the rationale being that if you give money away people tend to forget its value and perhaps use it irresponsibly – you need to ensure that they share the responsibility with you.

The other scheme I became very interested in was the purchase of a Lithotripter, a highly sophisticated instrument which dissolves gall-stones externally by means of shock waves, thus sparing elderly patients the trauma of an operation. Oddly enough the device had been originally developed by a German aircraft company, who had used the principles of the Lithotripter for World War Two fighter planes. Initially, medical application of the shock waves was confined to the treatment of kidney stones, but it soon became apparent that gall stones would respond to similar treatment. I was fascinated by the notion of this Lithotripter, and I travelled out to Munich with David to have a

120

look for myself. The cost of the machine, a prohibitive £1m, was way beyond the grasp of the NHS. Using my business skills, however, I negotiated the price down to 700,000. The Germans, used to dealing with doctors and hospital administrators, were fairly taken aback, I think! Later, when we were back in England, the Germans came over and we negotiated a final price at the Next headquarters in Enderby.

The Businessman's Responsibility

The bigger your company, the greater your responsibility to society. You can't simply feed off the community and then give nothing back, and at Next we became involved in many different charitable schemes. Far too many businessmen expect the Government to look after the social environment in which they operate. They complain about the degeneration of inner cities, when they should really be helping to tackle it themselves. They are, after all, the ones with the resources. I always felt this responsibility acutely, which is why Next was an early supporter of the Albert Dock scheme in Liverpool. Arrowcroft, the developer, with the help of David Phillips a local property man, had transformed the remains of the once busy dock into a fabulous development with offices, flats and retailing units. I felt that the place had enormous potential and that it would be of benefit to the local community. David must have thought that my experience as a retailer and marketeer could be used to promote the complex and draw in other retailers. I was very keen that our involvement shouldn't stop merely at Liverpool, for there were many other inner cities crying out for attention.

One of Next's happiest associations was with the Royal College of Art. There was, however, a brief period when the relationship appeared to be in jeopardy. Lack of Government funding meant that the RCA had had to seek private sponsorship of their various shows and degree ceremonies. Next staff – Frances Mossman, for one – lectured on the RCA fashion course, and it was therefore quite natural that we should take on the sponsorship of the RCA fashion show in 1985. It took the form of a fabulous gala evening to which the press were invited – all paid for by Next. I was therefore horrified to hear through the grapevine one day in February 1987 that the RCA were looking for further support for their annual degree shows and that they

121

had money from Burtons which they planned using. Joanne Brogden, Director of Fashion Studies at the RCA, tipped me off that I would also be getting a call from the college Rector, Jocelyn Stevens, and sure enough the phone call soon came through. Now, Jocelyn is known to be a difficult and acerbic man, and I hadn't yet met him, but I was so annoyed about the Burtons story that I immediately went on the attack, chastising him for seeking support from our competitors when we had been so loyal to the RCA in the past. True to character, Jocelyn's retort was as fiery as my own outburst. 'Look, I don't need a bloody lecture from you,' he bellowed, 'it's my job to find the money wherever I can.' Our conversation continued in much the same tone, but by the end of it I had suggested we meet and that further funds might be available from Next.

Jocelyn and I are now friends, I'm happy to report, and he wrote me a lovely letter after the sacking. I think he's done a marvellous job at the RCA, bringing some style and contemporaneity to the place. In July 1988 he conferred upon me a senior fellowship of the college which I received at the Albert Hall along with Joanne Brogden, Quentin Blake (water-colourist, illustrator and Head of Illustration at the RCA), John Halas (cartoonist and animator), F.H.K. Henrion (the designer) and Sir Denis Mahon (the art historian). I was in the best possible company, and was greatly honoured.

High Street Kensington and Department X

Despite the inauspicious timing of its opening, coinciding as it did with my father's last days, the High Street Kensington store was to become one of my favourites. It was the first major project I'd given Rasshied Din, a young designer from Manchester who'd worked as a freelancer with David Davies on earlier schemes and who'd since set up his own practice early in 1986. I first approached Rasshied in July 1986 with the proposal that he redesign the units at our South Molton Street and Knightsbridge ladies' wear stores. Rasshied did an excellent job (although he now claims it was the cheapest work he's ever done, but that he took it because he was desperate for the work!). When I asked Rasshied to take the project on, David Davies had already started work on High Street Kensington, but his designs, though beautiful, weren't going to give me the 'busy' feel that I'd first identified at Hermès in Paris, and which I now wanted incorporated into this store. I took Rasshied over to Paris so he could experience for himself the 'feel' that I was after.

Rasshied later told me that Kensington High Street nearly gave him a nervous breakdown. It was certainly an enormous task for a complete unknown, but the store when it opened was (and still is) wonderful. Being on the 'wrong' side of the street, in other words across the road from Barkers, the store had to be striking enough to attract customers over. Our bait was a large and theatrical window which took in both storeys of the shop's façade, and which was peopled (for the first time at Next) with elegant mannequins. We built a sandwich bar right at the front of the store. There's always a queue there that gives the bustle and activity I was seeking. Once inside, the decor is subdued and upmarket, with cream paintwork and much use of traditional materials such as terrazzo and timber. The merchandise is arranged so as to guide the customers around the shop in a natural and logical flow – men follow a route down one side of the store, and women go down the other. In June 1988, we were presented with a Royal Borough of Kensington and Chelsea Environmental Award for the architectural work on the frontage of the High Street Kensington store. It was well deserved.

Although we'd made a strong statement at High Street Kensington, the concept wasn't far removed from our original Next stores, and many other designer-type retailers had copied the look. I now wanted to do something quite different with store design, and having acquired a large Oxford Street site with the CES takeover, I had the perfect opportunity for a whole new image. At Next we had always fashioned our identity with the customer in mind; this new store, situated as it was at the young, Tottenham Court Road end of Oxford Street, begged for a brand new, contemporary design.

Our merger with Grattans had involved me increasingly in a new world of computerized warehousing systems, and it occurred to me that we could incorporate some of these hi-tech features into the design of the new store. With these thoughts in mind, I took Rasshied along to one of our warehouses and showed him the merchandise handling systems. I was particularly taken with the computerized carousel that brought merchandise to you at the push of a button, and there was also an amazing pater noster which brought up shoes in the style and size you had keyed into the computer. Rasshied brought both of these systems into the new store design, as well as many other ideas inspired by visits to our warehouses. Both the carousel and the pater noster would actually carry merchandise to the customer, just as they did in the warehouse, and they would bring movement to the store. Another source of movement were the transparent tubes we built into the store, through which batches of money would dart like rats throughout the course of the day. This was an ingenious way of despatching money down to the safe when the tills became full, and actually it was one aspect of the store that wasn't modern – years ago that's exactly how larger stores would cash the takings of each sale. The store was fitted out with industrial and warehousing fixtures, thereby creating a stark interior which complemented the high-tech systems. As for the merchandise, it was no different from that stocked in our other large stores, but for the first time ever we displayed it by product group rather than by collection – this seemed a far better approach for the younger market who do not want to have their outfits 'coordinated' for them.

We launched the new Oxford Street store in August 1988, along with a store in Glasgow designed and fitted in the same way. For months we had pondered over a name for the stores, labelling them simply 'Department X' while we tried to come up with something else. By the time a decision was imperative, 'X' had grown on us, so we stayed with it, although we lost it briefly when a Yorkshire clothing company called 'X' took us to court and won. On appeal, though, we won back our right to the name, and the distinctive 'X' logo was ours once more.

Both of the Department 'X' stores launched well, and certainly while I was at Next they were achieving a higher density of customers than any of our other stores. I remember the manager of the Oxford Street Department X ringing me to report progress, and remarking that the clientèle was quite different from what he'd become used to when managing the High Street Kensington store. Department X was, he said, the 'alternative Next'. It was a sentiment echoed, albeit more negatively, by Christ Hirst, a friend and Next supplier. 'I'm not at all sure about this new Department X,' he said. 'I much prefer High Street Kensington.' I knew then that we'd got the concept right. I wanted the Chris Hirsts to continue going to High Street Kensington. Department X had never been intended for them, it had been designed with a different customer in mind, and the stores' trading figures soon showed us that *that* customer approved. We'd cracked a whole new market.

Innovation was the constant theme of the seven years I spent at Next. The City's predictions for our future growth spurred me to come up with new concepts, but beyond that pressure was my own enjoyment of the creative process. In the early days of Next, I had channelled my creative energies into the merchandise and the image of our first concept; but I had moved away from the fashion aspects of Next, and become more heavily involved in store design and the use of space, progressing from the Reading and Romford stores through to the futuristic Department X stores. Then there was the Next Directory, which would upturn all those received notions about mail order, and which was a result of my belief that High Street space would become less available and more expensive. We were forever looking into the future. Most people follow, but at Next we led.

So it was that we became involved in BSB (British Satellite Broadcasting) in May 1987. For me, fashion retailing has always been as much about communicating as selling – we communicate so much to one another through the clothes we wear – so when we were approached by Granada and Virgin, the founders of BSB, we were immediately interested in Next having a stake in the new medium. Pitching my vision forward some four or five years, we could see a time when people in Britain would be ordering goods via their TV screens, and if that were to happen Next would be there in the vanguard. BSB offered us a seat on the Board for £20m, which we negotiated down to £10m. It was still a great deal of money, and there were many unknown factors involved, but the venture had all the right vibrations for Next and we could see the long term benefits.

125

The 24 Hour Shop

The last new concept we developed before my firing was the 24 hour shop, which we saw as the stage between going out shopping and ordering goods from home through the TV. Once more the idea came to us as a result of our efforts to get round the problem of rents. The advantage of a high rent pitch is that it will give you the rapid turnover you need to keep your stock moving; if you go to a small town, you may pay a lower rent, but your turnover will be much slower and from the point of view of stock control and distribution the operation becomes comparatively expensive. We wanted to get Next into these small towns – after all, nobody else was serving them – but how could we do it without the massive investment in stock that would be required for each shop? The answer was that we'd stock only one of each garment in each of the sizes. Customers could therefore come in, try the clothes on and then order their chosen items which they could either pick up the following day, or have delivered to their homes within 24 hours (hence the name). Local delivery would be free of charge. In effect, the 24 hour shop would never be out of stock. In a normal store you may run out of, say, size 14 dresses. You can always order more, but by the time they arrive, several potential customers may have already been in and out of the store, having not even had the chance of trying on the dress in their size. In the 24 hour shop, that dress would always be there. The other plus was that the garment actually bought came fresh from the warehouse, and had never been tried on by anybody else. The 24 hour shop was, then, a sort of half-way house between mail order and High Street shopping, and nobody had done it before. Our first shops opened in Haywards Heath and Skipton in October 1988, and the feedback from customers told us that they loved the idea. The potential to develop the 24 hour shops is enormous, and I'll be interested to see what the present incumbents at Next do with the concept.

9

THE SACKING

The Next Directory

The Next Directory was the fruit of our union with Grattans, and Next's first sally into the mail order market. Our launch date was 11 January 1988; by the end of that first week we'd received around 27,000 phone calls, and within four weeks there'd been more than 500,000 requests for the catalogue. Part of our success was the wonderful press coverage – we'd invited the press (both fashion and business) to a wonderful launch party in the Lloyds building. After drinks and a buffet, and a small speech from me, the doors behind me opened dramatically, and I invited our guests to walk through to a gallery of blown-up photographs from the Directory – the effect was quite spectacular.

Those anxious months back in 1981, when Phyllis Walters and I had struggled to arouse press interest in the ladies wear launch, now seemed a very long time ago. Everything Next did these days was news, principally because each of our new concepts was unique in its own way – we were innovators, and that makes good copy. The Directory was no exception to this rule. The day it was launched, it was described by Gail Rolfe of the *Daily Mail* as, 'The most talked-about book in fashion'.

We found that its appeal was so broad that we were able to give a different angle to each of the publications we spoke to: because it encompassed clothes, accessories, shoes, furnishings as well as household gadgets, the Next Directory was a business story, a fashion story, a City story and a home story – everyone wanted to cover it. I particularly remember being interviewed in my office by the BBC's Clothes Show, and that programme more than any got us off to an excellent start – apparently the phones at the Directory's Leicester headquarters went wild!

The Directory bore little resemblance to many of the cheaply-produced catalogues which had only ever served to confirm mail order's down-market image. The merchandise was of the same high quality as the rest of the Next product, and we used top models and photographers to display it in 350 glossy pages. As well as the pictures, we provided fabric swatches and a tape measure with each Directory, plus the promise of delivery of goods in 48 hours. All the customer had to do was pick up the phone, and order their chosen items. The order would go straight into a computer which would then check the customer's credit worthiness while he or she was still on the line. Within four hours of the call, the goods would be packed and loaded for despatch to one of our 300 distribution points, from which our couriers would deliver the package to the customer's door. Each Directory cost us £8, and we decided to charge customers a nominal £3, not so much to recoup our costs, but more as a marketing technique – I wasn't after customers who just wanted a free book, I wanted people who were prepared to give some sort of commitment, even though it was only £3.

The designer of the Directory was Tim Lamb, whom I'd originally met through Phyllis Walters and who had done graphics and artwork for the men swear concept. It was he who suggested Lynne Franks when we took the decision to hire a PR firm for the Directory. Since parting with Phyllis, Next had developed its own in-house PR operation, headed up by Annie Sharpe, but we felt that the Directory would be better served if information about it was released from a fresh source. We had had initial discussions with a number of direct marketing agencies, but it soon became clear that their way of working wasn't ours. Some proposed simply to bombard customers with magazine advertising, leaflets and so forth, and although statistically you're bound to get a response with that sort of marketing, it can be both expensive and inefficient. After various presentations we I decided to form our own marketing team, comprising Tim Lamb, Lynne Franks, Dick Swain (the Marketing Director at Grattans), and John Wallis from Kaleidoscope/Scotcade, a Grattans' subsidiary. Tim and Lynne had quite different views from the other two, but that didn't concern me at all: in any aspect of a business, I believe that a certain amount of tension is essential, and while Tim and Lynne provided the creative and more flamboyant ideas, John and Dick had a more practical influence. My job was to balance and exploit these superficially opposing, but basically complementary, elements.

We explored various marketing routes, and I remember going to presentations at three major London advertising agencies, but in the end we decided that our offensive was going to be PR-based. Lynne Franks appointed one of her account executives, Vicky Pepys, to handle the Directory, and I have to say she did a marvellous job. As in the early days with Phyllis Walters, I became very involved in the PR side of the Directory, working closely with Vicky as we planned our strategy, and making myself available to talk to the press. There was one hiccough that I recall, when one of my colleagues inadvertently leaked to *Marketing Week* a new name for the Directory. I'd always maintained a distant relationship with the trade press, mainly, I suppose, because I was interested in reaching the public, not colleagues and other retailers. The trade press always wanted the story first, but my feeling was that if you complied with them, you not only reached the wrong people, but you also ruined the story for the main press, which was where you really wanted to be. Anyway, *Marketing Week* said that we were going to call our new catalogue The Book. It so happened that we *had* considered this as a possible name, which, funnily enough, is the name Great Universal Stores gave to a catalogue they produced later. It was a minor incident in an otherwise excellent PR campaign.

That same January of 1988, I was voted Retailer of the Year by stockbrokers County Wood McKenzie. The Wednesday after the launch of the Directory, I went down to London with Liz and David Jones to attend the ceremony at County Nat West brokers, having no idea that it was I who had won the award. I hadn't wanted to go to London because that day there was a sales conference at Enderby, which was to be followed by a Merit Award ceremony, but Liz and David, who were both in the know, had insisted. I was anxious to return to Leicester, however, as I didn't want to let down the people at the sales conference, and especially the Merit Award nominees. We flew back from London early in the evening, and I remember that it was a very still night, because we were actually able to land the helicopter at Enderby, which we'd never done before. The word must have got out that I had won the award because as we approached the helipad, I suddenly saw about 200 people looking up at me out of the darkness – quite spontaneously they had all run outside to greet me. I was moved to tears, and will always remember that as one of the best moments I had at Next. Yes, I had won the award, but these were the people who had made it possible.

· The Directory was a fine product, but it had been hard fought for – I admitted this to Deyan Sudjic when he interviewed me for the *Observer* magazine at the time of the launch. But I went on to say, 'That's a good thing, because it means that it's going to be hard for anybody else to do. If you can do something in half an hour, then so can anybody else.' And that was – and remains – perfectly true. There was, however, a dimension to our battle to produce the Directory that I wasn't going to tell the press about, and it is perhaps what made it so special and unique. Within our project team we had people from Next who were strongly product- and customer-led, and Grattans personnel who clearly understood systems and operational aspects. Of course, there was friction but that was very healthy. I remember when we were trying to decide whether or not the Directory merchandise would be handled by Grattans' warehouses. David showed Liz and Frances Mossman round his warehouse. Whilst the system they saw was well planned, quick and efficient, it didn't meet the ideals of the two women. We had a lively debate but David Jones could clearly understand that the market was different and would require a different approach. David believed in what we were doing and helped resolve our differences. He was a great ally. It was only when he stopped believing in me that things would go seriously wrong.

Culture Shock

One of the key features of the Directory was the 48-hour delivery promise. While we at Next were responsible for the product, Grattans were the operations people, and they were therefore in charge of delivery. In the July of 1987, we held a progress meeting where I specifically asked if we were going to be able to fulfil the 48-hour promise, and I was told that yes, we would. In November 1987, two months before it was due to be launched, I held a Board meeting during which we reviewed in detail every aspect of the Directory. Again, I raised the question of 48-hour delivery: 'If I put in my order at 5 p.m. on Monday,' I said, 'will I receive the goods by 5 p.m. on Wednesday?' 'Yes.' 'Good. Now, if I put in my order at 8 p.m. on the Monday, will I get the merchandise by 8 p.m. on the Wednesday?' There was a pause, and then I was told, 'Ah, well that's more difficult . . .' 'But that makes 48 hours, doesn't it?' I asked, by now very angry. 'Yes,' was the reply, 'but the trouble is our Super Agents don't work in the evenings, so they would have to deliver on the Thursday morning, which is pretty close to 48 hours.'

As this conversation progressed, we all agreed that delivery was a key issue, and none of us was prepared to accept anything less than 100%. Our reputation was at stake. The Super Agents we had spoken about were Grattans' couriers, and it was they who were to be in charge of delivery, so I contacted Tony Kane, who was looking after Directory operations for Next, and asked him to arrange a meeting with the Leicester agents, the most geographically convenient group. Going into the Next lecture theatre to address people took me back to the Pippa Dee days, and I immediately felt at home. We had a friendly chat about the Directory, which they liked, and I then brought up the subject of 48-hour delivery. In the back of my mind I knew that I wouldn't go ahead with the Directory if we couldn't keep the 48-hour promise; Next was about quality and integrity, and once we began chipping away at our promises and backtracking on our claims, our reputation would be irreparably damaged. I therefore had to be tough with the Super Agents, and I put it to them that if they weren't prepared to do evening deliveries, I would have to take the work elsewhere. Evening deliveries it was.

I could now see that we would also have to take charge of the Super Agents' training, and tighten up the whole operation. The agents would be the customer's direct link with us, and it was vital therefore that they should both understand and reflect our philosophy of quality. It was six weeks before the launch, and we had no alternative but to pull our staff out of the training department, and send them round the country to meet the network of agents. We also decided to design a smart black jumper for the couriers, bearing the words 'Next Directory'. Shortly after the launch I remember receiving a note from a customer, praising the Directory, but noting that their courier had been very scruffily dressed. I immediately sent a memo to Tony Kane, asking him to investigate the matter. At Next we had high standards, and we worried about such details – it's the small things that make the difference between excellence and mediocrity.

You can argue that from the outset I should have called our union with Grattans a 'takeover', which is what it was, and not a 'merger', and that Next should then have imposed its culture on Grattans. But my reasoning at the time was that our deal was an amicable one, and that 'merger' was a friendlier term than 'takeover' – perhaps naïvely, I thought that the enthusiasm I shared with David Jones would overcome the cultural differences. Perhaps I thought too that having succeeded in absorbing Hepworths into our culture, I would be able to do the same with Grattans. I never was. While even with expansion, we at Enderby maintained our family culture, the people at Bradford worked under quite different conditions. The Grattans headquarters was a very different building, with uniformed commissionaires at the door and a top floor which was reserved for the directors. I especially abhorred the Directors' dining room, where only certain selected Directors were 'privileged' to eat. How different it was from our canteen at Next where we *all* ate. I was so proud of the hours worked by the team at Next. On reflection I can see that very long hours can have a detrimental effect, particularly upon your personal life, which is so important as well. My understanding is that such cultural differences no longer exist.

In the Balance

However, in spite of the local differences that occasionally arose we planned the launch of the Directory in a great atmosphere of excitement and anticipation. Responsibilities were allocated according to expertise. I have always believed it is imperative to use the talents available across a group. Within a month of the so-called merger, for instance, we closed down our computer sector at Hepworth House – the staff were either made redundant or absorbed into Grattans who were, I acknowledged, the experts on systems.

My approach was to think 'group' and I know that David now felt the same, although it did not always seem to be the case. At the outset, I had my worries when he would refer to himself as 'Chairman of the Grattan Board' and say that the loss of that Chairmanship would be the worst thing that could happen to him. He was naturally very proud of his achievements in Bradford.

In September 1986, just two months after we joined up with Grattans, Robert Cooper, Next's Finance Director, warned me of the difficulties in merging two groups, after an acquisition: I've seen many occasions where the power and control switches and the Chairman finds himself out. After the 'merger', the four executive members of the Board from Next were Robert Cooper, John Roberts, a Tom O'Malley of our credit card operation and myself. We were joined by three Grattans' men: David Jones, Peter Lomas (his Finance Director) and John Whitmarsh (Warehousing and Systems Director), both of whom had come with David when he'd moved from Great Universal Stores to Grattans. John Whitmarsh's appointment was discussed at length, and Peter Lomas's arrival meant that we now had two Finance Directors on the Board, which was pretty odd. However, David insisted they join us, and I gave in out of goodwill. I can see now that my belief in what we could do with Grattans overrode all other considerations, and I should have taken heed of Robert's warning. He was never happy about Grattans, and I remember arguing with him, and putting across my case: 'How else are we going to get the profits we need for the future if we don't go ahead with the mail order idea? And who else other than Grattans could we do it with?'

I think for Robert this was the final straw, particularly because I hadn't given him the support he expected, but I was motivated primarily by a desire to maintain good relations between Next and Grattans. Within six months of the Grattans' deal, Robert had handed in his notice. He could see that Next was going to become a different company from the one he had joined, and preferred to return to the City. With his departure, the balance on the Main Board changed from four-three to three-three.

Robert wasn't the only one to remark upon the souring of the atmosphere at Enderby. Inevitably, with the takeover of Grattans and then of CES, as well as our other acquisitions, I became increasingly distanced from Next. Because my concerns were now 'group', I wasn't as closely in touch with my team at Next as I had been, so I wasn't as aware as people like Frances Mossman, and Liz of the impact Grattans was beginning to have on our culture. While at Next the atmosphere had always been positive and confident, new influences were beginning to seep into Enderby. The Next team had never doubted their effectiveness, and even when confronted with the apparently impossible, we had always had the vision and the confidence to say 'we can do it'. But now all of that was beginning to change. Grattans' people would come down from Bradford and talk about the weaknesses in our systems and warehousing. We had never pretended that they were our strength, but some people felt that it was not helpful for our new partners to major on our weaknesses while we were going out of our way to major on their strengths. Of course I was aware of these problems, but I also knew that as Chief Executive, it was up to me to mediate and not to take sides. I wanted to be absolutely fair, and I still believed that Grattans and Next had a future together. Even today, without George and Liz Davies, they have the ability to be a unique and outstanding Group.

Like Robert Cooper, Tom O'Malley was now starting to feel uneasy about his position and, as he was in his early sixties, he decided at the end of 1987 to retire. Tom had joined us in April 1985 as Managing Director of our store card operation, Club 24, which was run from Hepworth House in Leeds. It had started out as a joint venture between Hepworths and Forward Trust, a finance arm of the Midland Bank, and for a long time there had been discussions about the possibility of us selling up our stake in the business because they did third party business for competitors like Etam. In fact, what eventually happened was that shortly after Tom arrived, Next began negotiating to buy Forward Trust's share of the business, and in September 1986 Club 24 became a wholly owned subsidiary of Next.

It was at that same time that David Jones's team from Grattans had taken over the running of the group's computer systems, which had resulted in the closure of Hepworth Computer Services. Tom wanted a new system installed at Club 24, and after some to-ing and fro-ing, it was decided that the Grattans' computer people would take charge of the job. A result of the decision was that David Jones became very closely involved with Club 24, and he soon began saying that he was very worried about the business's level of debt. I didn't doubt that he knew what he was talking about - Grattans' business was based on credit – and I was disturbed at the news. In any credit operation there will always be a certain amount of outstanding debt you write off at the end of the year, but David was saying that the level of debt at Club 24 was unacceptable. I trusted David's judgement in the matter, and knowing that he was far better qualified than I to deal with Club 24's problems, I appointed him Chairman of the subsidiary. After Tom had retired at the end of that year David brought in a new Managing Director called Arnold Iverson. We then took the bull by the horns, writing off the Club 24 debt to the tune of £13.4 million, thereafter adopting a more conservative approach to bad debt. Less than a year later, when I brought in Price Waterhouse to look review our finances, this was an area they looked at closely.

The retirement of Tom O'Malley also meant that another of the original Next Board members had departed. At the time, I believed his resignation was sad but inevitable. With his departure, I lost another ally on the Board. Liz had been appointed Product Director in the August of 1987, so the balance which had then reverted to four-three, in Next's favour, now became three-three once more. It was to make my position highly vulnerable.

Gathering Bears

Preparation for the launch of the Next Directory had been the main concern of the product team after the Grattans takeover, but now that it was off the ground, we turned our attention in March 1988 to the Grattans' catalogue merchandise which was in desperate need of revamping. David had always been very protective of the product, but when Janice Baker, who ran Grattans' ladies fashion department, suddenly left in early 1988, it gave us the opportunity to make a radical change. We agreed it was time to use Liz's talents to set things right. Liz was going to have her work cut out, because changing the product would also mean bringing in a new product team to replace the people who'd been doing the job so badly, and from May 1988 she began five months of working between Leicester and Bradford, while she shaped her plans for Grattans.

1988 was going to be a busy summer for all of us, as we prepared for the launch that August of the second Directory. Liz had just given birth to our first daughter, Lucia, and we decided in June to take a week's break in Aix-en-Provence. David and his wife Anne joined us for the last three days of the holiday, so that David and I could sit down quietly, away from the phones, and discuss our future strategy. We both knew that the future was not going to be easy, but during those few days our discussions were positive and the atmosphere relaxed and friendly. It was the calm before the storm.

We returned to England to prepare for the launch of Directory 2. We had set very high targets for the first Directory, and although it hadn't quite met them, we had broken a string of mail order records: 20% of our customers were men, as opposed to the normal 5%; while our return rates were lower than those of our competitors, our average order per customer was higher – within weeks of our launch, 48% of our customers had made a repeat purchase. By any standards, the first Directory had got off to a flying start – having cost £25m (including stock investment) to launch, the stakes had been high, but we had broken even. We had every reason to believe in the success of its successor.

We launched in August, and everything appeared to be going well. However, I then flew to Mauritius where we had a major investment in manufacturing, run by Denis Rivett. He is an outstanding man: when Liz and I first found the factory four years ago, while on holiday in

Mauritius, it employed 80 staff. By the time we left Next, Denis was managing 4,000 people! We returned from this latest trip full of optimism, only to discover that the second Directory was starting to underachieve. The Post Office had gone on strike, and initially we thought our business would remain unaffected, by and large, as 90% of our orders were made on the telephone. What we hadn't counted upon, however, was the psychological effect the strike would have on our customers. Although *we* knew very well that we had our own independent delivery system, many of our customers ceased to put in orders during that period, simply because they assumed our business would be affected. A further unfortunate result was that we got behind on recruitment of new customers, who were unable to send in the tear-off order slips from magazine adverts. Overall, the Directory managed to achieve some good figures during that second season, but the strike had cost us many millions in lost sales and it was now clear that we weren't going to make the targets we'd hoped for in our first year of business.

During that August the City was also leaning on us heavily, as we approached the announcement of our interim results. The whole of the retailing sector had been under a cloud for some months now, with consumer spending dropping just as the cost of retailing space was rising, and I was especially worried about the overall financing of the Group, with regard to our debt-equity ratios – particularly in view of the disastrous effect the postal strike was having on Grattans' business, and that of its subsidiaries, Kaleidoscope and Scotcade. We switched all our attention to these matters, and during the course of a business dinner with David Jones and Mike Stoddart (who had become a non-executive Director when I took over the Chairmanship), it was decided that David would assume responsibility for our financial management during this difficult period, reporting directly to me. Some months later David and I agreed to bring in accountants from Price Waterhouse to assess independently the nature of these problems.

The following month, on 27 September 1988, we announced our interim results. That day signalled the beginning of the blackest weeks during my time at Next. We had changed our year-end from August to January with the Grattans takeover – one of the two companies had to

137

change, and we felt that January was more appropriate for a retailing group. I knew that this was going to be a tough year, but events had conspired to make matters bleaker than we – or anyone else – had anticipated, and the knives now came out. In the words of Nick Bubb, a retailing analyst at Morgan Stanley, 'The bears have been gathering around George Davies all summer. Now they are dancing on his grave.' Our pre-tax profits for the 6-month period to July 1988 were increased by only 2.3%, at £30.9m, and with the announcement, our shares duly fell by 18p to 182p, and then by a further 9p to 173p – half the level of the previous year. There were many other sources of pressure on our profits, principally the fall-out of the CES purchase. During the year we had spent £30m converting the new stores over to the Next formula, and the expenditure had consequently pushed up our level of borrowing. This was further increased by the interest payments due on the Convertible Eurobond we'd taken out to finance the CES purchase, and which had gone so badly wrong with the October 1987 stock market crash. With the consequent drop in our share price at the time from 360p to 250p, it had become apparent that the guaranteed return that we had promised investors over time would have to be taken into account. We therefore had no option but to take out a £43m provision which was basically the extra interest payments we'd have to make. Over the coming 4½ years many other company's had taken the convertible European option and had suffered in the crash as we had, but we had a particularly hard time because our Eurobond was so large and because we were the first to have to explain our difficulties to the City. Interest rates on our other borrowings were also rising, and were a further source of anxiety.

In short, our situation was an uncomfortable one. In spite of the continued excellent performance of our High Street operations, we now found ourselves caught in a position where we were over-stretched and over-geared, just as consumer-spending was slowing down – in other words, our level of borrowing was far too high, and we were going to have to de-gear our balance sheet (i.e. reduce our debts) and rationalize our business interests. It was at this point that we took the decision to sell Salisburys and Zales to Gerald Ratner, for £150m – our view was that if retailing was going to become increasingly difficult, we would rather have the cash on our balance sheet, thereby reducing our borrowings. I believe that it was a good decision; Salisburys, we believed, had peaked, and we consequently got a good price for it. I understand that since then it has been struggling, and Gerald Ratner may now be wondering if it was such a good buy after all . . .

The day before our half-year announcement in September, we held a Main Board meeting where we discussed how we would proceed with Liz's plans to overhaul the Grattans' product. It was agreed that the first step would be to move ladies' wear down to Enderby, and that other ranges would follow in the coming months. David said that as we were the product people, it might be more appropriate for me to come up to Bradford and explain to the staff that there would be major changes. I agreed. I knew that I would have to handle the situation correctly, because otherwise people would feel insecure about their future, and I had therefore taken care to talk through our plans with both the Grattans' and Next Personnel Directors, as well as Stephen Smith, who was Grattans' Buying Director.

I arrived at Bradford early in the morning – about 8 a.m. – and as I walked into the Grattans' building, I bumped into Dick Swain, Grattans' Marketing Director and a long standing friend of David Jones. 'How are you feeling,' he asked me, and I replied that although I wasn't particularly looking forward to telling the product staff of our plans, I was sure we had come to the right decision. 'I'm not so sure,' he said. 'What the hell are you talking about?' I said, 'We've been through all of this.' 'Well,' said Dick, 'you know, Next hasn't got such a good infrastructure, has it?'

I made my way to David's office, incensed by Dick's remarks, and reported the conversation. Instead of dismissing Dick's negative sentiments, David said that he wanted to talk about the overall strengths and weaknesses of the Group. He said he was worried about certain aspects of the Directory and whether Next, as at Enderby, had the infrastructure to handle the transfer. I couldn't believe my ears and totally disagreed with what David was saying. Surely it would be better to have the Next team develop and approve the product allowing Grattans to concentrate on their expertise in systems. For the first time I felt unsure of my ground.

Having gone through the change in detail with Stephen Smith (Grattans' Buying Director) the previous Friday, I felt confident that he at least would support me, and I therefore said to David that we should call him up and see what he felt about our plans. Stephen arrived, and to my surprise, he too had suddenly changed his tune and was now saying that he was against the move away from Bradford. He felt a few weeks later to join Freemans Mail Order.

I was angered by Grattans' sudden turn around, and I closed the meeting, declaring that I wasn't prepared to waste any more of my time (or Liz's) on Grattans' product. On my way back to Enderby I phoned Liz and John Roberts, and asked them to meet me for lunch. The morning's events had upset me enormously, and I wanted to talk them through with people I could trust before returning to my office. Liz in particular was now going to have to undo all the preparatory work she had done for the move over the last five months, which had included creating a new team of buyers. What amazed us both about David Jones's decision was that he had always been a great fan of Liz's and had been at pains to tell the City that Liz was coming in to improve the Grattans' product. After he had changed his mind, he avoided her and I don't think they spoke again other than at Board meetings.

Two days later, I phoned David and said to him that our joint responsibility lay in keeping the Group together, and that if he wasn't happy with our plans for the Grattans' product, then we wouldn't carry them through – there was no point in arguing about the matter. David was delighted and described my decision as 'statesmanlike'.

In October Liz wrote a report explaining that as a result of the decision at Grattans, she could no longer be held responsible for the Grattans' product, although she was Group Product Director. The report was presented at an Executive Board meeting we held in early November, during the course of which there was a bit of a rumpus. While I was out of the room, answering a phone call, it was said that there had never been any final agreement at the previous Board meeting about the plans for the Grattans' product. Liz disagreed vehemently and had a flaming row. When I returned to the room I could tell from the silence and the atmosphere that there'd been a fight, and when we came round to discussing the previous Board Meeting, I simply said that I saw little point in thrashing out the matter any further. What was done was done. Grattans could keep their product in Bradford. We agreed, however (and this was minuted) that as Liz and I were the experts on product, no product appointments would be made without our involvement, just as we wouldn't appoint any computer or systems staff without consulting David. This was particularly relevant at the time, because Stephen Smith had left and there had been some discussion about whom we should bring in as the new Grattans' Buying Director.

The following Tuesday, I learned that David had appointed to the position a man called John Williams. I got straight on the phone, and asked him what the hell he was playing at: 'We agreed only last week that you wouldn't appoint anybody without talking to me first, and now you've gone and done it. It's not that I'm totally against your choice, but we can't carry on running the business this way.' David then proceeded to deny that we'd reached any sort of agreement about recruitment of product staff. To be fair to him he had to do something to resolve the product situation at Grattan, but when emotions run high, the smallest things take on gargantuan proportions. The whole situation was getting out of control, and in a bid to restore unity I turned to our Main Board non-executive directors, Mike Stoddart, Jeff Rowlay and Brian Marber. I explained that the divisions had widened to such a degree that we were reaching a point where the two camps could no longer work together. We had to find a solution. And fast.

A Diary of My Last Days at Next

(Friday 25 November 1988)

We had a useful Main Board meeting today. where we pursued the possibility of splitting the two companies apart and retaining the Directory as a joint venture. I've had this in mind as a possible solution to our troubles for the previous six weeks. Asda and MFI have done it, so I don't see why it shouldn't work for us. David and I discussed the idea beforehand for a good two hours with Brian, Jeff and Mike (the three non-executive Directors), explaining the factors that had brought us to this position, including the basic cultural differences of Next and Grattans. It was a bit like going to a marriage guidance counsellor! At this unofficial meeting it was resolved that David and I should go away and try to seek a way in which the two businesses might continue to work together. If we do decide to stay together, we agreed that Group Finance should be restructured as David has had to cope with the additional stress of sorting out our finances. If, on the other hand, we see no alternative but to split, the restruction would not be necesary. It was a very civilized discussion and I feel quite optimistic that we can find a way forward. After these discussions, we went into the official Board Meeting, which I chaired. Everything went fine, and we all agreed that David and I should sit down together and work out the best way forward.

I've just come back from John Roberts's house, where I went for a quick drink after the meeting – we've been pals for years and it was nice just to sit and talk through the problems with him. He said the funniest thing to me. We'd been chatting about Next and Grattans and he said that he thought a split was the only answer. When I replied that I really wanted to try and hold the group together, he said, 'You know, George, you're a powerful man and people are afraid of you.' I reminded him that I wasn't the only one: 'Chris Hawkins (Next personnel manager) tells me you terrified him at the Staff Council the other day.' I don't think John liked the idea that someone had complained to me about him behind his back, because the atmosphere between us suddenly became quite tense. I'm sure it will be OK, though.

Sunday, 27 November 1988

Liz and I went round for coffee at John's and Anne's (John Roberts and his second wife). We all got along fine, so I feel much better about that conversation on Friday.

Monday, 28 November 1988

David came down to see me from Bradford this morning, and said he really felt the businesses shouldn't split. He suggests I should step down as Chairman and that he and I should be Joint Chief Executives. I am reminded of a conversation we had last week when David said to me that Liz and I were such great innovators that we should work only two days a week, and spend the rest of our time sitting on a beach and dreaming up new ideas. Anyway, I asked him who else agreed with his proposal that we should become Joint Chief Execs, and he said, 'Oh, everyone at Bradford, as well as some of the people down here'. 'Well, who do you mean? Liz? John Roberts?' 'Not Liz,' he replied, 'but John, yes.'

As soon as David had gone I went straight round to John's office. I was quite calm when I walked in. 'John,' I said, 'do you think I should step down as Chairman of the group?' John waffled some sort of vague reply. 'I'll ask you again,' I said, repeating my question. John looked awkward and then came out with, 'That's a mega question which I'd need notice of'.

Later today he came into my office and said that he was happy with the situation, that I shouldn't worry and that I had his support. But suddenly I don't know if I can count on his support any longer – it's a terrible feeling: he looks under tremendous. I don't feel that close to him.

Tuesday, 29 November 1988

Paul Deacon (a retail analyst at Goldman Sachs) rang this morning and said he's going to put us down for profits of £90m for 1988. I don't think it's correct to mislead these people, and therefore said I could not accept his forecast, particularly in the light of our recent sales of Salisburys and Zales, who achieved the majority of their profit in the last 2 months.

I fly to the Isle of Man this afternoon to visit our store and to make a speech to the local business community on behalf of the Commonwealth Games Association of the Isle of Man.

Wednesday, 30 November 1988

I returned from the Isle of Man this morning to discover that a number of analysts had also been contacting David. I then phoned Paul Hamilton of Rowe and Pitman (our stockbrokers) who advised it would be appropriate in the circular that is about to be issued to shareholders advising of the recent proposals, to give a statement on current trading to put a stop to the rumours.

I'd arranged to meet Nick Bubb of Morgan Stanley this morning in Leicester. I didn't want to postpone the meeting, but I felt unable to talk as openly as I would have liked. I explained that the Class I circular was about to be released. Nick remarked to me afterwardes that I was clearly depressed and had given off negative vibes, but that I'd played his questions with a very straight bat. He's going to reduce his forecast from £90m to £85m. I feel very bad about not being able to give Nick more information.

David, John and I flew down to London this afternoon and worked on the statement with our stockbrokers till 9 p.m. It will be released tomorrow, to appear in Friday's papers. I was aware at that meeting that the atmosphere had changed – something funny is going on.

John is behaving very strangely. He came into my office this morning and asked if he could have a word with me. 'What is it?' I asked. 'I'm frightened of you. You scare me, George. There, I've told you now.' I asked him what on earth he was going on about, and he continued in much the same vein. 'I'm frightened of you, and I've come to a decision: if I have to go, I'll go.' Is he trying to tell me something?

Thursday, 1 December 1988

David and I have spent most of today fielding press enquiries about the statement. We said that our profits for the year to end-January 1989 would be 'significantly lower', and warned investors of modest growth for next year. The City analysts are now forecasting profits of £70m, and our share price has accordingly dropped 20p to 136p. These are pretty depressing times.

We've also had some further discussions with Ian Brindle and Glynn Barker from Price Waterhouse, about how we can weld the group back together. Liz and I flew down to London with Ian and Glynn this evening – we plan to have a few days off. As we dropped them off on the way to our house, Ian said to me, 'You're an open guy, George, and I think you ought to be more careful. Not everyone's the same as you.' I invited them in for a drink, and we talked further. 'Next is nothing without you,' Ian told me. 'Look, we've seen the way you work, we've spoken to your people, and we know how you relate to them, I'm now on my guard.

Friday, 2 December 1988

The press reports this morning seemed quite fair and I get the feeling some people are disappointed. I had planned to have a day off, but cancelled it to give interviews to press. David rang me and was very upbeat and friendly. He suggested it might be a nice idea and a show of confidence if we were both to be seen buying Next shares now that we've made our announcement – I agreed, and have bought 100,000. David has bought a further 150,000 for himself and John Whitmarsh.

Tuesday, 6 December 1988

It's been good to have a couple of days off after last week – but I don't think this week's going to be much better. I've a strange feeling of unease this weekend. As I was driving to the London Zoo this morning [I am a non-executive Dirctor there] I had a call from Steve Lowe. He sounded very worried. 'John Roberts had me in his office for a very long time last Friday, asking me what I thought about you and about the group. Then David Jones rang me, and began talking about the Chairmanship. I didn't want to give them the wrong impression, so I said very little – but I feel very worried.' I told Steve to put his thoughts in writing, and send them to John, so that there could be no misunderstanding about his loyalty to me.

What the hell is John Roberts up to? I rang him this afternoon, and was told he was watching the Varsity match on T.V. I then decided to pop in on Brian Marber [a non-executive Director of Next], and learned that he was actually at the Varsity match.

Wednesday, 7 December 1988

Lunch today with the Marks and Spencer Board – Rick Greenbury, Nigel Colne and David Sieff. We had a really good talk about our style of running a business, getting involved in the product and so forth. I took John Roberts along with me, and as we left, John apologized for not being in his office when I called yesterday. He looked a little flustered. I looked him in the eye and said, 'Listen, I know you've had a word with Steve Lowe, and I don't want to know the reasons why. But just remember that you and I are friends, and I never let my friends down.' He got into his car, and I got into mine.

I flew back to Enderby this evening for the Directory Christmas party. I had a lovely surprise when I arrived, because unbeknown to me all the senior directors at Next (save those on the Main Board) had laid on a special surprise reception for me. They wanted to show that in spite of our flat results, they were totally behind me. I'm very touched. I then went on to the Directory party – there was no other Group Board member there, which is odd.

Thursday, 8 December 1988

Paul Hamilton [Next's stockbroker] arranged a series of meetings with the City institutions today. David was nowhere to be seen, although he was supposed to be making the presentations with me. It was a long and tiring day, and with immaculate timing, I was passed a telephone message as I left my final meeting with Sally Clifton at the National Provident Institution. It read: 'Ring Mr Stoddart or Mr Rowlay at Slaughter and May.' I'd been up since 5.30 a.m., and I'd made presentations to more than fifty people, but my mind was now racing. *Why should Jeff Rowlay, the Leeds-based non-executive be at Next's solicitors without my knowledge?* The events of the past few days flashed through my mind, and I suddenly saw with absolute clarity what was about to happen.

I picked up the phone, dialled Slaughter and May and was eventually put through to John Roberts – so *he* was in it too. 'We want to call an emergency Board Meeting at 8 p.m., but Mike and Jeff want to see you on your own first. Can you contact Liz, and make sure she comes to the meeting as well?' I listened quietly to all of this, and then came back with, 'John, you and I have been friends for a long time. Are they trying to do something to me?' As usual, John prevaricated. 'Well . . . probably, George . . . but Mike wants to talk to you, so he'll explain.' I pushed him no further. 'Fine, John. Don't worry about it – I'll get back to you later.'

I hung up, and immediately began to wonder what was the best course of action. Should I go to this meeting? Or should I avoid it? The first thing, in any case, was to call Liz and tell her to get down to London right away. And now what? Suddenly I felt terribly alone. I knew that I needed a solicitor, and quickly, but now for the first time I found that the one I had always relied upon – John Roberts – was no longer there for me. I phoned another solicitor I knew of in Birmingham. No joy there either. It was now 7 p.m. Perhaps I should go to the Battersea heliport, where I knew that the men from Price Waterhouse, Ian Brindle and Glynn Barker, were arriving shortly? I could tell them my story. They understood me. They would support me. I made my way over in the Rowe Pitman [our stockbroker's] car. It had seemed simpler to use it today, but I now wished for my own car, and Kevin Jones, my loyal and trusted driver. Maybe Rowe and Pitman were in this too? I told Ian and Glynn that I believed I was about to be fired. 'Don't be silly, George,' said Ian. How I wished I shared his confidence. We returned to Liz's and my house in Oakley Street. I phoned Mike Stoddart. 'I appreciate we have a problem here,' I said, 'but I'd just like you to have a word with Ian Brindle before you take any hasty action.' Stoddart spoke to Ian, but refused to be persuaded against an urgent meeting that evening at Slaughter and May. Ian now agreed that my fears were well-grounded.

He got on to his boss, Alan Wheatley, and told him what had happened. Alan was extremely helpful, and put us in touch with a solicitor – David Freeman of D.J. Freeman – who was just leaving his offices for the day. We then drove to Price Waterhouse, where we awaited Liz's arrival. She was driven down by Kevin. When we arrived at Slaughter and May, I noticed that our other Next driver, Harry Poulton, was parked outside. Did he know something too? Was that why he gave Liz and me our Christmas card yesterday? At 9 p.m., six of us – Ian, Glynn, David Freeman and a colleague of his called Jonathan M. Lewis, Liz and I – arrived at Slaughter and May. We were ushered into a room to await our fate. Michael Stoddart, Jeff Rowlay, John Roberts and the Company's solicitors presently came in. Stoddart seemed to be in charge. 'It is more in sorrow than in anger that I have to say this, George,' he said, 'but we have come to a point in the business where it's going to have to be run differently. You've been a brilliant leader at Next, but reluctantly we now feel that the time has come to part company with you, and with Liz too.'

David Freeman had told us that he would do the talking, and he now said: 'What are your grounds for taking this action? Has Mr Davies embezzled company funds? Are you accusing him of stealing anything? What has he *done?*' They agreed there were no such accusations. He then continued: 'Gentlemen, I have no intention of working through the night, and I suggest we put a moratorium on this for the next fourteen days.' We left the room, while David Freeman had a few words with Mike Stoddart et al, and the Slaughter and May solicitors. He then came out to tell us that although the solicitors were happy to delay the matter, my Main Board wanted us fired tonight.

10.30 p.m. Liz and I entered another room where we found assembled the full Board of Next (with the exception of Brian Marber, who was in Hong Kong) – David Jones, Jeff Rowlay, Mike Stoddart, Peter

Lomas, John Whitmarsh and John Roberts. There we went through the macabre motions of a Board meeting. Our colleagues voted us both off the Board.

It was now 11 p.m. Just a few minutes later Liz and I had left Next for ever.

10

THE LESSONS OF NEXT

Public Support

Dear Mr & Mrs Davies,

I write as a very grateful fan of Next, to say 'thank you' for bringing top fashion (but not top prices) to hundreds of satisfied customers like me. I have many outfits from Next with which I have been delighted; they represent excellent value, style and workmanship.

My friends and I feel very strongly that you have been treated most shabbily after all your efforts in putting Next at the top in fashion. We wish you both well for the future – and hope you get adequate compensation, which you so justly deserve!

V. Riddington, Gumley

Dear Mr Davies,

Shocked and disgusted you've been ousted. How can somebody else take over Next? You are Next. . . . They are the losers, George, not you. Go for it, and stay my hero in the business world.

A. Mitchel, Leicester

Dear Mr Davies,
Your concept for Next, and its amazing success, make you a true star in re-
tailing history. I hate seeing you treated this way, but am now sitting back and
waiting to see what your brilliant mind and outstanding business acumen will
lead you to do next.

J. Dawson, Winchester

Dear Mr Davies,
I take this opportunity to salute you, and acknowledge that without a shadow
of doubt Jones, Stoddart and co will live to regret their actions, and that as
surely as the sun rises in the East and sets in the West, you will *be successful*
again and again.

G. Owen, Leicester

Over the weeks that followed that dreadful evening at the offices of
Slaughter & May, Liz and I received some 2,500 letters of support,
many of which were from total strangers – such as the above. There
were also letters from suppliers and members of staff, all expressing
their shock at our dismissal. I quote from just one of these, written by a
Next shop manager: *'Next will never be the same company without the two*
of you at the helm. All I can say is that for the past three years I have worked for
you, and I have been proud to do so. Knowing you, I expect there are many new
plans that you want to put into practice, so come on! There are a lot of us loyal
ones out here ready and waiting!

We felt it was most important that we shouldn't put pressure to resign on friends who remained at Next. We didn't want people leaving
their jobs for us, with nowhere else to go. Two of our dearest friends,
however, did just that, and the day that I learned of this was the only day
during the whole saga that I was moved to tears.

I will never forget that day. It was about a week after the sacking
when Frances Mossman telephoned me at Oakley Street, and asked if
she might come round and talk to me. We sat on the sofa together while
she told me that she had had a discussion with David Jones that morning. She had said to him that because of the events of the previous
week, she no longer felt able to continue at Next. 'What about

Andrew?' I asked her. 'He's resigned too.' I knew that Frances and Andrew had financial difficulties, especially as they had recently adopted their first child, Tomas. Their courage and loyalty was, and remains, very precious to Liz and me.

The phone didn't stop ringing either, and one of the most memorable calls that came through was from Robert Maxwell (whom I hadn't met at that stage), and who said to Liz, 'Give a message to George. Tell him it's better to know the shits today than to work for them for the next 20 years.' Many other people whom we admired and respected spoke out publicly about their disgust at the way in which Liz and I had been treated by our fellow Board members. Terence Conran, I remember, said in *Retail Week* that I had been made a scapegoat for Next's problems. He went on: 'In sacking George and his wife, the board have disposed of the company's greatest assets.' Nick Bubb, the retail analyst at Morgan Stanley who had become a personal friend over the years, also decried what had happened: 'I think they have thrown out the baby with the bath water,' he told the press.

Newspapers speculated about what had happened, many of them homing in on the fact that David and I had both bought shares in Next just days before I was ousted, and suggesting that I was the victim of a political-style coup. Having been advised by David Freeman not to speak to journalists, we released the following statement: 'Mr & Mrs Davies informed the Board of Next plc at a Board Meeting which took place at 11 pm on Thursday December 8 that in their view there was no justification for their dismissal from the company. D.J. Freeman and Co have today issued proceedings against the company for wrongful dismissal.' David Jones and Michael Stoddart were free to speak to the press, and in an article in the *Sunday Times*, David was quoted as saying: 'George's style is basically unstructured and I believe people need clear lines of responsibility, firm direction and the ability to say to someone, "I do not agree with you".' In the *Observer*, meanwhile, Michael Stoddart said: 'It all came down to a philosophy of management, it's structure and reporting methods. His strengths of a few years ago are now not appropriate for a company of our size. If he had been prepared to listen we would not have reached this position.'

I have always had good relations with the press, and during those difficult days, I was buoyed up by the feeling that in spite of what they were hearing from Next, the journalists remained sympathetic to Liz and me. Nick Bubb, the Morgan Stanley retail analyst did his best to present our case to the city press, while Kathryn Samuel in the *Daily Telegraph* spoke for the fashion press when she said, 'None of the exaggerated epithets so common in the fashion business are quite adequate to describe the shock waves that reverberated through the industry at the news of George Davies's removal from the Next board. Davies *is* Next. For good or ill, it cannot be the same without him.'

Such messages of goodwill helped us through a period of shock and confusion. Liz and I never imagined that it would come to this. I had had no fears for my position, because I hadn't believed the City would ever accept my dismissal. I had expected that they would understand that we had built a business, that it had grown at an amazing rate, but that it wasn't possible to keep up such a rate, especially at a time when the retailing industry as a whole was slowing down. This was a matter of common sense, but of course what I came to realize was that greed, not common sense, rules in these situations.

Naturally, in my wildest dreams, I could never have predicted that this would happen to me. Some people have said I should have seen it coming, but it is easy to be wise after the event. My loyalty and affection for people sometimes outweigh my better judgement, and I hope that I have learned to be more cautious now. I started out feeling a great deal of anger and bitterness towards my old friend John – only three years previously he had stood beside me as my best man when I had married Liz – but now I am simply saddened by his actions. He must have his reasons, but I will never understand them.

Perhaps I was naïve as well to expect an outraged reaction from the people in the City I had worked both with and for. Of the 2,500 letters we received, not a single one issued from the institutional investors for whom I had made so much money in the past. There were no phone calls either from these people who had fêted me so very recently, and I have to admit that I found that painful. Ironically, Next shares actually dropped 5p to 128p with the news of Liz's and my departure; earlier in the week they had rallied on the back of rumours that I was planning a management buy-out. But you learn in these situations that loyalty is a rare commodity, and where once I had been the toast of the City, I was now most definitely a *persona non grata*.

The Short-Sighted System

There is no mystery as to why this had happened, and although I was initially very upset about the actions of the Board I quickly identified the fault as lying in our system. In Japan, success in business is assessed on a long-term basis, where increasing your market share is judged to be of greater significance than the short-term profit. This set-up allows the entrepreneur to develop and to take risks in doing so, and it means that your results are viewed in the context of the whole of your sector, and not in isolation. In the UK, however, we are judged on our day-to-day profits, a very short-sighted and damaging system. The slump in Next's fortunes was to be mirrored across the sector – our misfortune was that we were among the first to inform the market. While I had danced to the City's tune, meeting their ever more ambitious forecasts, I had been their blue-eyed boy. But once that growth took its inevitable toll on our balance sheets, our shares came tumbling down. What the 'schoolboy scribblers' (as Nigel Lawson once described the City) didn't seem to understand was that you cannot keep on fulfilling potential, and growing *ad infinitum*. It's the same in any business – if you have a restaurant with a maximum capacity of sixty, you can continue serving more people until you have filled these sixty places, and then you have to stop. I was perhaps foolish in that I provided an astonishing rate of growth, fuelling expectations that nobody would have been able to fulfil. It's actually quite interesting to look at what Anita Roddick has done with the Bodyshop – she's developed at a gentler rate, but one which is still quite acceptable to the City, and she's therefore dealing with a different level of pressure.

During the first few weeks after the firing, I felt an all-encompassing anger towards the City, and swore to myself that never again would I put myself at the mercy of analysts and institutional investors. But gradually, as the shock subsided, I began to see the City in perspective, and I understood that it was unfair to tar the whole system with the same brush. It's that small part of the machine – the fund manager, making money out of the buying and selling of shares – who tends to give the system a bad name with people like me. The City comprises scores of different disciplines, and over the past few months I have learned that many of the top people in the City institutions also have strong reservations about the way in which fund managers operate, and the market instability their decisions provokes. To be fair on the fund managers, their performance is assessed every month, and they are under tremendous pressure to achieve the short-term gains that I am arguing against, but I suppose I did feel that I *had* served them well in the past, and that I might have heard from one or two of these people when I parted company with Next. Whatever, I am now far more circumspect about my relationship with the City, and having gone through the pain of feeling personally rejected, I have reached a position where I feel that it is the short termism of the system that is at fault, and not the individuals.

There *is* something in the British character which makes us highly suspicious of success. Perhaps that's really where the root of the problem lies. I remember that after we'd announced our disappointing interims in the middle of 1988, I was savaged in a particularly vicious *Retail Week* article. Our profits were still actually climbing, albeit at a steadier rate, but the magazine homed in on the fact that the Next phenomenon was slowing down, and attacked me personally. The piece was headlined, *GEORGE LOSES HIS GLAMOUR LOOKS*, and described Next as beginning to look like '*the adventure playground for G. Davies.*' It went on: *Now the fun must stop . . . George Davies has enjoyed himself enormously, and very publicly, in the role he cast himself as retailing's mister creative. Perhaps there was a hint of self-indulgence in the way he sped, in his helicopter of course, from the Next department store to the Next Directory, to Next Jewellery and the Next nursery. But who could begrudge jovial George his obvious delight in the business when sales were rocketing and his clothes were winning plaudits from the fashion pages? He had become a legend in his lifetime. But so did Judy Garland.* Here was a publication which lives by and represents the retail trade, and yet the impression was that for seven years it had been waiting for me to make one false move, and that it was now crowing. The article's effect was deeply damaging both to Next and to me. Its negative sentiments began to spread, infecting the rest of the press who hitherto had been highly supportive of us and of the way in which we were dealing with our difficulties.

I don't know why it is that we treat successful people so badly in this country, but I do know that it's an attitude that has made us highly defensive in business. We smother our entrepreneurs when we should be nurturing and encouraging their talents. Sir Clive Sinclair is an example of somebody I admire enormously, and who is treated as something of a joke in this country. He has brilliant and daring ideas, like his little C5 car which sadly never took off. Today it seems obvious that the car could solve some of our traffic problems in central London, and who's to say they won't pedestrianize London and suddenly create a need for the C5? The point is that sometimes an idea can be too revolutionary, too ahead of its time. In America, achievement is applauded, and even if you hit a bad patch people remember your success. Over here you can almost hear the cheering when the mighty fall.

I've said that we're defensive in business, and what I mean by this is that our approach is to hang on to what we have, rather than striking out in new, innovative directions. I call this the corporate attitude, and I now suspect it's the way many businesses are being run today. My experience with the Ashington factory, described earlier in this book, serves to illustrate what I'm talking about. The non-entrepreneurial, corporate decision would have been to close down the factory, thereby defending the rest of the business from the drain of a non-productive operation. I argued to keep Ashington open, and once we had adapted production to the needs of the 1980s, the factory became highly profitable. Clearly, my route required more effort, and it was also a risk, but risk and effort are what success is all about. The Ashington story also discredits the notion that the successful entrepreneur is wholly a greedy and self-seeking individual, a misconception which unfortunately flourishes in this country. By adopting an entrepreneurial approach to the problem, we saved 400 jobs.

I think Margaret Thatcher has attempted to encourage a new spirit of entrepreneurialism in this country, and there are more and more small businesses which are challenging the old corporate order. But we will have to be very wary that our ingrained caution and cynicism do not extinguish the light. I have fought many battles on this front in my time, and on reflection, it sometimes looks as though my greatest achievements were born out of adversity! I remember the problems we came up against when we wanted to expand into manufacturing. I was told it would be expensive, difficult and time-consuming. I recognized all of that, but beyond the sweat and the endeavour, I could see the logic of total involvement in the manufacturing process: not only do you control the quality of your product, but you also know that all of your ideas are coming back to you, and not being sold to competitors who happen to use the same supplier. Furthermore, if you have a master plan, you can make a far better concerted attack on the market.

What Next for Next?

It is my fervent hope that Next retains its position that was characterized by the very special award we received in March 1988 for development through innovation.

Businesses normally reflect the personality of the people who are at the top of them and no doubt the future Next will be the reflection of David Jones and Michael Stoddart.

I have noted that in the last few months, two further businesses have been sold – Dillons/Preedys for £53.9m and Mercado for £10.7m. They have announced that there will not be a follow up to the Garden Directory and I have received a circular informing me of the sale of Suttons of Wisbech who operate in the Horticultural market.

In April this year I received a heartbreaking letter from the staff of Next Gardening Directory, imploring me to help them save the business from closure. The Gardening Directory, a brainchild of Lesley Jones, Liz and I, was launched a month after my departure from Next in January 1989. The Gardening Directory was a good product and I would have loved to be involved in its launch. I felt very sad when I received this letter but, in fairness to the new Next management, their strategy had to take account of the wider available resources and the interests of the Group today.

We at the grass roots of the venture feel that it has not been given a fair run. The Directory has been operational since 26th January 1989. Since that date, orders have been steadily increasing to the point where we now have two articulated lorries a day arriving at the site to collect packages. These lorries leave

156

the site full to capacity . . .

The letter continues:

Due to the short time span between the start of the operation and our visit by Mr Varley [MD of Next Directory, and the man who brought the news of the Gardening Directory's imminent closure], *it seems that the decision to close must have been taken very soon after the venture began, and obviously cannot be based on current turnover.*

We understand that the Directory was originally your 'baby', and feel sure that you, at one time, were certain it would succeed. We, in turn, are certain that in your hands and with our joint determination it could still be very successful.

Please will you help us?

Autocratic?

Eight years of devotion and love of one company was summarised in the Annual Report: 'It was apparent that the management style that had been successful in a small environment was not as suitable to a group of such diversity. It was, therefore, agreed that we should dispense with the services of George Davies, Chairman and Chief Executive, and Liz Davies, the Group Product Director.' I would be lying if I were to say that I wasn't hurt by these few curt words. When the Report and Accounts actually appeared the January after my firing, they recorded pre-tax profits of £62.3m, which was much lower than brokers' prediction. The retailing arm of the business had actually picked up, and the shortfall was due to Grattans' figures coming in at an incredible £10m lower than we had anticipated. Throughout the months that followed our sacking life was very difficult for us. There is little to be gained in dwelling upon the details of what we experienced in our legal battle with the company we had once lived for. I only mention this matter by way of warning to anybody who is dismissed as we were. Suffice it to say, any contract you might sign when you join a company is only worth the paper it's written on, and you need to steel yourself for some painful and nasty wrangles if and when you are dismissed. For the record, I'd also like to note here that the law appears to have been created for lawyers, and not the clients they are supposed to represent.

Although Jones and Stoddart had given their reasons for sacking me

157

as my 'autocratic' and 'unstructured' management style I felt very sad that Liz had to go too. Liz was, and still is, the most talented product developer that I have ever worked with. Because of my high public profile, it was perhaps inevitable that the majority of sympathy was focused on me, and the only person who showed more concern for Liz the day after we were fired was Alex, my 15-year-old daughter. 'I can understand why they did it to you, Dad,' she said when she telephoned us, 'but what can be their grounds for doing it to Liz?' Liz was very touched by Alex's concern, and since that day there has been a very special bond of friendship between them.

Like most other people, my other older daughters, Melanie and Emma, first heard of the firing on the 8 o'clock news the following morning. By midday they were both with me, having leapt into their cars and driven down to London from Nottingham, where Melanie is taking a degree in Business Production, and Manchester, where Emma is studying Retail Marketing. It meant a great deal to me to have them there, and I cannot overemphasize the importance of strong family ties in moments of crisis. My mother is another person who has given us enormous strength in the last few months. Paradoxically, her anger at the way we were treated actually had a positive effect on her, reinvesting her with the fighting spirit that was diminished by my father's death.

While the fashion world, the City, the press and the public speculated about the whys and the wherefores of events at Next, I did some very hard soul searching. Next's fortunes had taken a downward turn during 1988, and as the company Chairman and Chief Executive during that period I had to take a long look at my own actions and examine the tough accusations that had been levelled at me. Had I failed to supply Next's management needs? Was I indeed autocratic? And should I have adopted a more conservative approach to expansion?

There is no easy answer to any of these questions, but if the clock were to be turned back, I would almost certainly do things in the same way. My abiding memory was of this unbelievable pressure to meet the City's extraordinary forecasts, which started out as an exciting challenge, but which eventually became an uncomfortable treadmill. In my first year after joining Next, the group announced profit figures in 1982 of £3.9m, which had risen to £92.4m by 1987, with analysts predicting figures of £125m in 1989, and £150m in 1990. It's also possible that I would still be at Next if I had settled for a gentler and less aggressive growth curve over the years; on the other hand, however, that course of action might have laid us open to the attentions of aggressive predators.

It's fair to say that with our expansion, Next grew away from the principles upon which it was founded, and during the latter months it became a massive corporation which bore little resemblance to the 'family' we had started out as in 1981. I chastise myself for failing to maintain the grass roots contact I had had with our product team in the early days, but given the increasing corporate demands being made upon me, I cannot see how it could have been otherwise. I suppose that if I were to identify a crucial error on my part, it was that in my love of the product and marketing I failed to attach the same importance to administrative functions. My advice to a budding entrepreneur is, whilst recognising his own personal strengths, that he should take great care in the selection of people for those areas with which he cannot be so closely associated. You need decision-makers in every area, otherwise the burden becomes oppressive and dilutes the effective use of your own talent.

In a note to me in October 1988, Nick Bubb suggested that City neurosis with regard to Next stock was exacerbated by our failure to communicate with investors. Ironically, of course, I had spent the day of my firing in a series of meetings with the institutions, explaining our policy and plans for the future, but I have to accept that clearer channels of communication might have been established had I appointed an Investor Relations Director. And it goes without saying that such an appointment might have prevented the negative views that the City can adopt if one is not at their beck and call every minute of the day. David Jones always tried to shield me from the incessant calls. I remember one Friday afternoon when David had to take over 17 calls, purely to talk to analysts responding to a totally unfounded rumour on the Grattan's Autumn/Winter catalogue. They have got to realise that while you're talking to them you're not making money for them. Most analysts remind me of the old bookies' runners!

Looking back over my relationship with the City, I can now see that the real problems began with the stock market Crash of October 1987. At the time, I think we underestimated the effect the Crash would have on our business. We realized, of course, that it was disastrous from the point of view of our £100m Eurobond issue – what had once seemed an excellent idea had now saddled us, along with Tesco, Argyll and Storehouse among others, with the prospect of redeeming the bonds in five years' time at a price 33% higher than the original issue price. But I don't think we understood until much later that the Crash was to have a further very insidious effect on Next. Up until that day in October, our share price had climbed and climbed, but now for the first time it nose-dived along with the rest, and we were suddenly seen to be vulnerable. The bull market optimism that had accompanied our glorious ascent was wiped out overnight, to be replaced by neurosis and pessimism.

In the New Year of 1988, in spite of our excellent results, City commentators began to criticize us for the first time. Their confidence in our figures was marred by the belief that our acquisitions had left us too highly geared, and burdened with crippling interest charges. With the announcement of our interims in September 1988, relations with the City hit an all-time low, our results were tarnished by the £43m interest provision we had taken out on the Eurobond, and the postal strike had dealt a body blow to profits from the Directory. I responded to the situation as I would still respond today, by reducing our gearing from 125% to 50% through the sale of Salisburys and Zales to Gerald Ratner later that October. The move was unfairly interpreted as a 'panic sale', when in fact it was part of a long term plan to reduce our borrowings.

But the final straw was when I was forced to make that ill-fated announcement in December, warning investors that our 1988/9 profits were to be 'significantly lower' than the previous year. Institutional investors in the main do not behave as private investors, who have a deeper understanding of the long-term aims of a company. Short-termism is the name of their game.

The electric rate of expansion took its toll in many different ways. My team at Next found it increasingly hard to pin me down, and this they found demoralizing. In recent conversation with a journalist, Frances Mossman, one of my key product people, said: 'We used to be able to get hold of George at any hour of the day – his door was always open. He made us feel that we could achieve anything through hard work, and Next was the most amazing place to be. It transformed people's lives. But as the Group grew larger things had to change. In the past everything had been achievable, but now doubts were beginning to creep in, and George's time was increasingly taken up by the City and the Group's corporate needs. If George had been a more ruthless person, the situation would never have evolved as it did – to a more wicked person, it would quite simply never have happened.'

This last point of Frances's appears to contradict the 'autocracy' of which I was accused by David Jones. Was I autocratic? In a sense I was, if by 'autocracy' you mean that I had high standards, that I cared about the business and that I was a decision taker. After my firing, Irvine Sellars (Chairman of Ford Morris Sellars) said to me, 'Frankly, George, if you aren't autocratic, you shouldn't be running a business.' And I believe there's some truth in that. Somebody at the top has got to be prepared to take ultimate responsibility, otherwise you end up running your business like the Civil Service or a golf club – by committee, in other words. My detractors say that many of the staff at Next were afraid of me, and that they are relieved that I am no longer to be seen stomping around the building and checking up on what's going on. I find this hard to believe, for I was always approachable and deemed to be one of the best motivators around. I did indeed move in on departments that weren't functioning well, and could become quite passionate where I saw incompetence and waste, but I never lost my temper and I never went in for personal criticism – it is simply not my way. Had that been the case I would not have been able to build the loyal and talented team that made Next what it was.

My commitment to Next meant that I felt responsible for every part of the business – that's the Chairman and Chief Executive's job, I would have thought. Throughout my time with the company, I stayed at home every Saturday night, waiting for the trading figures to come through on the computer Liz and I kept in our bedroom. Sometimes, we would sit over the machine until two or three in the morning, so that we could start the new week with a comprehensive picture of our standing on the High Street. That level of devotion to the business was reflected throughout our team at Next, and although it could be tough, it also had its rewards. Frances Mossman put it this way: 'Working at Next could be very hard and exasperating, but it was also tremendous fun.'

I can give another example of my style of management. Early in 1987, I invited our Dublin store manager, Ronnie Reilly, to come over to England and tour some of our stores. We had hired a small plane for the day, and as we were heading for Newcastle, Ronnie said to me that I really ought to come to Dublin soon, and see how they were running the operation there. As it happened, I had wanted to do so for sometime, but had always been advised against an Irish visit because of security problems – when you're making people a lot of money, they tend to wrap you up in cotton wool! Anyway, on this occasion, I turned to Ronnie and said, 'I'll tell you what, do you fancy going now?' I then tapped the pilot on the shoulder and asked him if there was any chance of taking a left and heading for Dublin instead. Ronnie was astonished and delighted, but no more so than his staff in the Grafton Street store when the pair of us walked in that lunchtime.

So these are the sort of things that I did. There are two styles of management: the first I abhor, for it is about caution, and about removing yourself from blame when things go wrong; the second is about sticking your neck out, providing strong leadership and taking responsibility for your decisions. This second approach is essential if you are going to create something new and exciting: the alternative is about mediocrity. I remember reading many years ago that somebody had charted the fortunes of a series of businesses which had been built up by an individual – it had emerged that all of those businesses had started to decline once that individual left, taking with him the inspiration. The danger, of course, is that if you *are* that individual, you will be held personally responsible for both the successes and failures of your enterprise; while mediocre people survive simply by keeping their heads down, the entrepreneur will always be in danger because he takes risks and is prepared to put his name to them.

In my case this was especially so because of the high profile I achieved in the press. I was fully aware of the fact that the personal hype could turn against me should anything ever go wrong, but I also knew that both the press and the public liked me and that identifying me with Next was an effective way of promoting our product. After the events of December 1988, David Jones said to *The Times* that he was looking forward to the end of the personality cult: 'We recognize that Next is known as George Davies's Next. I hope and pray it will never become known as David Jones's Next.' What he failed to realize was that the public actually enjoyed seeing a familiar face at the head of the company, instead of the usual grey-suited and anonymous corporate façade. As for the press, you only have to look at the extraordinary level of coverage we attracted over the years to be convinced that my personality was an asset to Next.

I have never been a great player by the rules, and I think that has actually been my strength rather than my weakness in business. My disregard for hierarchy enabled me to strike up friendships with staff at every level of the company, and inspire both dedication and achievement. At the end of the day, you have to look at Next results and ask yourself, would another style of management have achieved so much in so little time? The answer to that question is the only justification I need.

My belief has always been that there is little point in raking over the past, wondering how things might have been, and dwelling on the pain of rejection and betrayal. In spite of what I created, I left Next with very little in terms of money. I was only ever a salaried employee, with a few shares. But I have emerged from the whole Next experience richer in many other more important ways. Among the letters I received after Liz's and my sacking, there was one from a former employee of CES, who lost her job as a result of our takeover of the group. I quote part of it: '*Maybe you will never be on the actual bread-line but I trust you will suffer some of the feelings of rejection and injustice that you inflicted on so many lesser mortals. . . .*' I certainly did suffer those feelings, and I think that the treatment I have received at the hands of my former colleagues has made me far more sensitive. A business isn't a charity, but you have to try and do the best for everybody – I will never forget how I felt that night in Slaughter & May.

There were many other lessons I learned at Next, which I will talk about in the context of my future plans, and in the course of writing this book I have had cause to reassert what I said in an early chapter, which is that my career has been a continuing business education. I have now come to regard Next as another phase in that process. Next achieved so much during those eight short years that it is sometimes hard to pinpoint our greatest success. But I suppose that for me it has to be the way in which we managed to change the world in our own small way. With the original Next concept we began a process of transforming not only the High Street, but also the British public's level of taste. With the Next Directory we persuaded the consumer that mail order didn't have to be downmarket. Through our policy of invention and innovation we actually *changed* people's attitudes, and in my opinion that is what true entrepreneurship is about.

This sense of achievement is mine, and it's something no one will ever be able to take away from me. Along with my memories of the fun I had building the retailing phenomenon of the eighties, it's what persuades me that the eight years I spent at Next weren't a waste of my time.

11

WHAT NEXT?

New Challenges, New Values

Ian Caldwell has been working on my mouth regularly over the last three years. He became my dentist after I walked through a plate glass door in South Africa, smashing my teeth in the process. In spite of the obvious handicaps to our relationship, we have become firm friends, and shortly after the firing, we met up for dinner. 'To be quite honest,' he told me that evening, 'I'm delighted they sacked you.' He went on: 'Look, I know it sounds awful to say this, but the pace at which you were working would have made you a sure candidate for a heart attack sooner or later. Leaving Next is the best possible thing that could have happened to you.'

Now that I have gained a perspective on the events of December 1988, I can only agree with Ian's words, which I confess were more difficult to accept at the time. What at first had appeared to be the end of the road, gradually revealed itself as an amazing opportunity to do something new and even better with my life: I hadn't lost out at all, for Next had fired me at my peak, freeing me from the burdens of a company that had grown away from the principles upon which it had been

165

founded. Contrary, therefore, to what one might have expected, the months that followed my departure from Next were a period of enormous personal confidence and excitement about the future.

I was greatly helped in my recovery from the shock by the immense amount of press attention Liz and I received during those early weeks. Everyone seemed to want to know what our next move would be, and at the time when our confidence was at its lowest ebb, it was wonderful to see that we were still very much considered a force to be reckoned with. I remember a spate of rumours in February and March that linked my name to Nazmu Virani's manufacturing business, Stylo. The story appeared in *The Sunday Times*, accompanied by a picture of me, and the following day Stylo shares shot up by 25p! This would have been all very well had I actually been involved in dialogue with Virani, but the fact is I wasn't and I was a little irritated to see how my name had been used to make other people money, when I hadn't gained a penny. I felt as I imagine a prostitute must feel when her client does a runner! I cannot deny, however, that it was gratifying to see the City's confidence in me returning.

There was much speculation, too, about the possibility of my heading up a consortium to take over Next. Within days of my departure from Next, *The Sunday Times* was suggesting: '*[George Davies] is said to be thinking about starting up a new company in direct competition to Next, or even mounting a bid for the company using his international contacts.*' *Today* also picked up on the rumour, and there's quite a story attached to that: I'd popped into the Next shop in Richmond one afternoon, and had barely been there for two minutes when one of the junior managers, who must have recognized me, came over and said that a phone call had come through for me. 'This is very odd,' I thought as I made my way to the back of the store. 'Who on earth could possibly know I was here?' The caller turned out to be a *Today* reporter, who wanted to know if I intended buying Next back. He refused to reveal how he had traced me, and to this day it remains a mystery – some of these newspapers have amazing networks of contacts, and I can only think that somebody in the shop must have provided the tip-off. I *had* in fact considered a takeover bid, and I was approached by various people with this in mind, but in the end I knew that I wouldn't be going back to the Next that I had loved, and that in any case far more would be gained from moving forward, rather than backwards: life should always be about looking ahead. My life had changed, and it was time to take on a fresh set of challenges.

Right from the moment I was released from my commitments to Next, I was presented with an array of extraordinary job offers. After receiving his phone call, I went for coffee and a chat with Robert Maxwell, who was highly supportive, having survived a similar experience himself. I was also contacted by Andrew Lloyd Webber, who I believe was looking for a new chief executive. This was some 24 hours after my sacking, but I'd evidently retained my sense of humour, for when his secretary came on the line, I asked her if they really thought my voice was good enough! I never actually managed to meet Andrew Lloyd Webber, because he changed our appointment three times, and in the end I got a little fed up and decided not to bother. Many other individuals and major companies wanted to talk to me. I had lunch with Richard Branson, who I think has been very wise to take his group private again. I also had some preliminary discussions with Geoff Mulcahy of Woolworths. The House of Fraser resurfaced again, too, and I did a little tentative work for my old friend Ali Al Fayed. The Hobbs group wanted to see me, as did Wilfred Cass of Moss Bros, and I also entered into discussions with Asher Edelman, who was stalking Storehouse at the time – I remember receiving an enraged phone call from Terence Conran at my home in Leicestershire, two days after Edelman and I had had our 'secret' meeting.

None of these approaches seemed quite right for me, but they had the combined effect of keeping me very active and focusing my thoughts on the future rather than the past, and for that I remain extremely grateful. One idea that I did pursue, however, was a golf club project that was suggested to me by my dentist friend, Ian Caldwell. Ian's an ex-Walker Cup golfer, and he found out about some land that had become available in Burford. While I was at Next, all my creative energies had been channelled into the company, but now that I had the time, I was able to take a long look at golf courses and the leisure industry in general, and put together a proposal along with Ian and Lesley Jones, the gardening expert who had helped us with the Gardening

Directory. We felt that most golf clubs were archaic: for a start, they are notoriously difficult to join, as well as being prohibitively expensive. But we also believed that the days were gone when the husband goes off to play golf, leaving behind his wife and family. What people want now is a complex where other activities for the whole family are available – riding, swimming, a par-three golf course, and so forth – and there are very few of those around. It's been tremendous fun working on the idea; fashion is a short-term, fast-moving business, and I've enjoyed the opportunity of developing a concept which has greater longevity. We hope to begin work on the course later this year.

A further scheme I became involved in was also in partnership with an old friend, David Phillips – the property developer with whom I'd worked on the Liverpool Albert Dock development. I've already mentioned my interest in shopping malls, and my concern that many of them are not fulfilling their early potential. My view is that the landlords have failed to create the right retailing ambience, and in so doing they have also failed to attract the retailing names that will draw in the custom. David and I both believed that the sagging fortunes of the British shopping mall could be transformed if only a more retail-orientated approach were adopted, and we had entered into discussions with two major City institutions who were interested in backing us. Tragically, those discussions never progressed beyond the preliminary stages, because one evening in May this year, David collapsed and died of a sudden heart attack. He was playing golf with his son, and had reached the third hole of the Formby course, which is about as far as you can get from the club house.

David was a month older than me, and he was always so full of life that for a long time I found it impossible to believe he had actually gone – even now I find myself thinking from time to time that I must consult him about something or other. Death can be very hard to believe. David's certainly threw many things into perspective for me, and I had cause to recall and agree with Ian Caldwell's delight at my departure from Next. My lifestyle during those eight years had become increasingly unbalanced, and many of the things I had cared about – my friends, my family, my recreational activities – had suffered at the expense of the business. They now returned to the centre of my life as I dealt with my past and considered my future.

When you are in a position of power and influence, it is difficult to judge the motives of those who appear closest to you but now that I had left Next I began to rediscover the joys of real friendship. Someone may call you a blood brother, but don't always believe them. My Liverpool friends immediately rallied round us. David Phillips was one of those who were among the most supportive, and both he and Hugh Smythe – another old friend – took me out for dinner a couple of days after the firing. Hugh is one of those people who has never had great personal ambitions, and has never sought the limelight for himself, but who has always been a rock in my life when things have gone wrong. I admire him more than almost anybody else I know. I met him all those years ago in Crosby, when I was a teenager, and we've shared a few adventures – not least of all, spending the night together in a single bed when we were 18! A crowd of is had travelled down to Spain that summer, and while everyone else opted for hotel accommodation, I decided that I would take my tent. This was all very well until the skies opened, heralding the arrival of the most horrendous thunderstorm. There was no option but for me to curl up with Hugh – he's never let me forget it! In later years, we would always play golf together with other friends from the Formby Golf Club. We formed a team and would go every year to play in Scotland against Prestwick. There was one occasion after the match when I challenged one of the Scots to a midnight race of two laps around the hotel at which we were staying – the distance was about a quarter of a mile. Unbeknown to me, he'd actually run for Scotland, and although I shot off ahead of him at the start, he was set to overtake me as we completed the first lap. As I made a spurt to regain ground, my legs gave way beneath me, and I fell headlong to the ground. Who should be there to pick me up and brush me down but Hugh Smythe! Later that evening, I had my revenge when I challenged the same fellow to do a flick-flack, which is a kind of backward flip. This competition took place in the hotel lobby, and I was judged the winner. I had had to give up the golf tournaments and the attendant silly games some three or four year as ago, when Next began demanding more of my time. Leaving the company made me realize just how much I'd missed out on while I'd been there, and I determined that never again would I allow my friendships and hobbies to be excluded in such a way.

A New Vision

Not only did I suddenly have time to reassess the values in my personal life, but I also found myself enjoying the luxury of looking in at the world of retailing from the outside. Because I was no longer tied by the demands of a business, I was able to let my mind wander freely, and I entered a new phase of intense creativity. As in the old days, when I had researched the original Next concept, I went out on the street and absorbed information and impressions, until I began to feel a vision for the future emerging. Let me try to illustrate how this works: I know, for instance, that the day of the dress will return before very long. I am sure of this because I have been round ladies wear shops talking to sales-girls, and whenever I mention dresses, the response has been, 'Every-one wants dresses, but you can't buy a decent dress anywhere, can you?' At the moment it's coordinates everywhere – Next is responsible for that – but people are becoming bored by that look, and I can gua-rantee that it's on its way out. The trick is to go back to the consumer first, to identify his needs, and then to bring out products which answer to those new needs *before* the public realizes that it has them. In the case of the dress, once I've established that that is what women will be demanding in the future, the next stage is to go to Liz who refines that vision and shapes it into a product idea – she has the most extraordinary knack of identifying the look the fashionable but ordinary woman is after.

Whatever I did in the future, I knew from the outset that I would want to keep it reasonably small, and that quality would be an essential ingredient. One of the businesses I looked very closely at, and which seemed to meet both of these requirements, was a small tile shop in Wimbledon called *Galerie 7*. Audrey and Frank who ran the business, and who had approached me soon after the firing, were wonderful people, and I felt right away that they shared many of my views on re-tailing. They had a high level of taste and they loved and understood their product, and further more, they saw – as I did – a growing con-sumer demand for stylish and exclusive tiles. They wanted to expand the business – not into a large empire, but into a small chain where all the quality controls could still be maintained. During the course of our discussions, however, I began to feel that deep down they were much happier with their single shop. Many people talk about expansion when they have a small business that's doing well, but in the end, not everybody is prepared to take the risks.

My reasons for wishing to stay relatively small in the future are a direct result of my past experiences at Next. There's not a shadow of a doubt in my mind that the character of businesses change fundamentally when they grow into a large corporation. Once you get that size you spend most of your time setting up systems and then administering them, and you lose touch with your roots. I don't think that the best things always come out of highly formal situations. The danger is that management becomes remote from the key issues that create the true wealth of the company. Does this have to be the inevitable result of expansion? In my dealings with garment manufacturers I've witnessed the same process, and that's why I now always favour the smaller manufacturer, where the quality of the product is paramount.

Quality is one of the most difficult things to achieve, because it relies on human intervention. A diamond, for example, only becomes a thing of beauty when it has been expertly cut and polished. I am now convinced that the standards I require are only achievable and maintainable when you have a small and close-knit team – apart from anything else, good people like Liz don't grow on trees. The philosophy of quality is embedded in me, and it was certainly part of my thinking at Pippa Dee, where we knew that our sales force would simply refuse to handle goods that they deemed to be substandard – it was a tremendous discipline. But in fact I think my concern with quality was born earlier than that, when many years ago, during my Littlewoods days, I visited a shop in the Avenue Louis in Brussels called *Du Jardin*. It was (and still is) the most amazing childrens' wear store I'd been to in my life. What impressed me even more than the exquisite clothes was the way in which the interior was designed to reflect the season's particular theme. I especially remember an elephant motif on the pyjamas which was repeated as a large wall hanging. I got into the habit of travelling over to Brussels every six months or so while I was a children's wear

171

buyer, just so that I could absorb the atmosphere of excellence. I can still see the little navy blue dress with a white piqué collar for 2-3-year-olds which I copied for Littlewoods, probably at a fraction of the price! Quality doesn't have to be expensive, as we proved during the early days at Next.

A further aspect of my plans for the future was that whatever I ended up doing, I felt sure that I wanted to be self-employed. This instinct was partially tied up with my desire to run a smaller, quality-orientated business. I believed that as an employee, I would have less control over the growth of the business and its standards. But I also knew that I would be far more able to concentrate on running the show if I was out of the City's eye.

Gradually, then, over the weeks that followed my firing, there emerged a picture of where I wanted to be in the future. I saw myself heading up a tightly-knit team of individuals, who not only shared both my belief in quality and value, but who believed in putting the requirements of the customer first. The next step was to work out how, where and with whom I could make this vision reality.

The George Davies Partnership

Fate has a funny way of making things happen in your life when you least expect it to, and the idea for my new venture arose out of a casual conversation over dinner between Liz and Geoffrey Carr, the Development Director at Asda stores and an old and loyal friend. Geoffrey was interested in Liz's opinion of the improvements Asda had made in recent months, and that evening he'd invited her to come and have a look round the Slough store. The day she was due to go, she mentioned to me her plans, and as I was doing nothing else at the time, I decided to go with her. It was a good while since I'd been into an Asda store, and as we walked in, I was struck by the transformation in image.

Asda stores are large out-of-town hypermarkets which date back to the fifties. They started out as discount stores, with the emphasis being on price rather than quality, and they were therefore always seen as a cheap and downmarket alternative to the High Street. Now, however, Asda had evolved into a more sophisticated concern, and the impression given by both the goods and their presentation was of quality. I was especially excited because for some time I had been sure that out-of-town was the big thing for the future. My gut feelings are often based on statistics, and I knew that the escalating cost ratios on the High Street would encourage more retailers to look to the out-of-town option. I've already spoken about my other concerns for the High Street, and how I feel it's becoming an unpleasant environment for anybody to shop, especially if you have small children with you. And quite apart from the dirt and the violence of so many City centres today, there is often the additional problem of parking and then the inconvenience of carting your purchases back to the car, which may be some way away. There are other unforeseen hazards too. When Liz and I went to Harrods recently, with our small daughter Lucia, we were told that we were forbidden to enter with a pram!

Out-of-town shopping appealed to me because it eliminated all of these worries, and now at Asda I saw that quality was becoming part of the formula, along with value and convenience. The one area, however, that struck Liz and me as being of a lesser standard was the clothing. We spoke about this to Geoffrey, and discovered that in spite of the inferior quality of the merchandise, Asda's annual sales on clothes was nearly £150m. How much more they could make, we thought, if they could only upgrade the ranges! If people were happy to buy their clothes at Marks and Spencer, what was to stop them from coming here? Once you'd actually arrived, the style of shopping was exactly the same, it was only the concept that needed improving. Geoffrey was interested in what we were saying, and suggested we meet the group Chairman, John Hardman. He and I hit it off right away, largely I suspect because we are both Liverpudlians, but also because I was full of respect for the changes John had made to the group. I didn't beat about the bush when I gave my opinion of Asda's clothing range, and I was quite forthright in my recommendations. I recognized that the public held preconceived notions about Asda clothes, based on the company's history. I believed, however, that now that out-of-town shopping was coming of age, the time was ripe to inject style and quality into the merchandise. A new look, combined with a vigorous marketing campaign, would draw the customer. It was a challenge, and it was one that I found enormously exciting.

What impressed me throughout my dealings with John Hardman and his team at Asda was their openness to suggestions from me, an outsider. He immediately arranged for me to meet his Trading Director, Bill Bailey, and his Chief Executive on the stores side, Graham Stow. Once more, there was an instant rapport based on shared backgrounds: Graham and I actually started work together on the same day in the same department at Littlewoods, and both he and Bill were also Liverpool-born. There followed a series of further talks with Geoffrey and John, which resulted in Liz and I signing a consultancy agreement with Asda at the end of February. The plan was that we should spend two months researching in depth the market and the concept for a new clothing range. In April we would then present a potential plan of action which would include not only designs for the clothes, but also the finer details of shop layout, display and packaging.

Early in March Liz, Geoffrey and I flew over to the USA. We travelled from Boston to New York and then on to Connecticut. From there we flew to Dallas, finishing our tour in Atlanta. At each destination we would head for the supermarkets, the hypermarkets, the out-of-town superstores, absorbing as we went our impressions of these vast shopping emporia. This type of retailing was a whole new ball game for both of us, and before we launched into creating a new fashion concept for Asda, we had to identify and understand the particular elements that made these large stores work. As I had learned all those years ago on that Littlewoods course, you have to start with the big picture before you move in on the detail.

It was a crucial point in this instance, because any clothing concept we developed would only work if considered in the context of the whole store; even the very best ideas would be as nothing if they were tucked away in a cramped space at the back of the store, or if the level of service was poor. If we were going to have to persuade the consumer that there was nothing peculiar about getting in the car with the kids, driving a few minutes out of town and buying clothes under the same roof as the week's groceries, we were going to have to make sure that the whole ambience was right.

These matters were all included in the presentation we made to Asda at the beginning of April. When we moved on to the actual ranges, we stressed that the key was exceptional value combined with wearability: quality clothes, in other words, that combined comfort and style with competitive pricing. Having analysed the market, we had concluded that across the board the Asda customer was really no different from the High Street shopper. We noticed, however, that there were demographic differences from one store to the next, and we proposed counteracting this by creating targeted ranges for the different stores. Another feature of the concept was that throughout each season, we would introduce new items to the range, in order to prevent the customer from tiring with the clothes on sale. This is something we had done at Next, and it gives you the flexibility to react to changing trends. Although the clothes within each range would be linked, there would be less emphasis on the coordination for which Next became so renowned. Our argument was that the customer had grown out of the coordinated look, and that possessed of a new confidence, he or she was now more interested in putting together a more individual look. This confidence was manifesting itself in other ways, and would be to our advantage when it came to persuading people to shop with us. Shoppers were no longer slaves to the designer snobbishness that had once persuaded them that a plain T-shirt, bearing a designer label, was worth £50. Their priority was now 'value', and they could see that it made more sense to buy exactly the same T-shirt for a quarter of the price at Marks and Spencer. Or, indeed, at Asda.

Critical to the realization of our concept was that I should have around me the right team of talented individuals. Just as I had done when I had moved to Pippa Dee and then to Hepworths, I made it quite clear that I would not be able to transform Asda clothing ranges without my people beside me. As I have said I am good at establishing a broad vision of where I want to go. But in producing merchandise of excellence, I then need, together with Liz, people of the same standards, visions and aspirations. The team I have today is quite outstanding.

The Board of Asda was impressed with our concept, and we entered into negotiations about how our relationship would work. It was important for me that I should remain independent, as in the future I would want to provide a similar service to other groups, as well as developing my company in new directions. I recognized, however, that Asda had effectively handed over their clothing department to me, and that it was only right to allow them a major stake in my enterprise – their holding is actually 20%, while Liz and I own a controlling 51% of the business. Other shares are owned by GDP staff, and two of our founding partners are Kevin Jones and Anne James, who have been outstanding in their support for Liz and me. Their belief in us remained unwavering throughout the most difficult of times, and they both felt unable to stay at Next after we left.

The George Davies Partnership (GDP), as we have called ourselves, is a new style of business. The key to our philosophy is that mutual effort and responsibility reap mutual rewards, and this belief is the foundation of our working relationship with Asda. As an independent company, supplying Asda's clothing needs, we are superficially similar to the traditional department store concession – in other words, all those names like Jaegar, Alexon, Mondi and so forth, who rent space in the large departmentals. During the course of my research into departmentals however (I spent some considerable time during the New Year looking at House of Fraser stores for the Al Fayeds), I identified a number of major flaws in the department store/concession relationship. Department stores aren't as attractive as they used to be, and one of the main reasons for this is that the presence of all the different concessions contributes to a very disjointed effect. The department store acts merely as a landlord, renting out the space, collecting its percentage of each week's takings, and taking no real interest as a retailer. The concession, meanwhile, is concerned only with its few square feet of the store, and it has no input on how the rest of the store might be organized so as to improve its own sales. In short, there is no real *partnership* between the departmental and the concession.

The relationship between Asda and GDP will show that there is another, more effective, way of operating concessions. My principal aim when I set up the Asda deal was that both partners should share an interest in and responsibility for the new concept. My starting point, then, was that GDP would only begin to make any money when profits on Asda clothes began to climb above the figures the group is currently taking on its ranges. I figured that if I were merely to take a cut of whatever we made, there would be little incentive on either side to improve sales above their current level. For Asda's part, the motivation would be there to take an interest in promoting our sales, rather than simply sitting back and taking their cut. By saying that GDP will only reap the rewards of sales made over and above Asda's current levels, we have demonstrated that we are committed to making the clothing concept work, and we have also established an ambience of cooperation. The benefit for us is that we are consulted about wider decisions concerning the whole store, but which also affect us – it goes without saying that the success of our new product will depend very largely on the image projected by the rest of the store. The working formula that we have come up with, then, ensures commitment to the concept from both parties, and a shared sense of responsibility, without any loss of independence on either side. When I look back over the years, I can see that establishing this sort of relationship in other situations would have saved me a great deal of hassle and heartache. For example, our mistake with Tricia Guild, when we were developing Interiors, was that there was never that mutual involvement.

The New Markets

Marketing the concept is a challenge I'm really looking forward to. In a sense, I'm starting out with a blank sheet of paper once again, because I'm confronted with a public who retain a downmarket image of out-of-town fashion, and I'm going to have to persuade consumers that clothes can be bought out-of-town as successfully as food and consumer durables. As I've said, true entrepreneurialism is all about changing attitudes, and that's where the excitement of this new venture lies – if it were easy, there wouldn't be as much fun. Somehow I will have to convince the convincers – the fashion media – of my belief that this is where we are heading in the future. I believe that the market is going to divide into two segments: on the one hand you'll have stores like M & S and Asda where you can buy highly wearable, highly attractive and competitively priced garments; on the other hand, there will be the one-off designer stores like Browns, where very expensive and more exclusive goods can be purchased. The consumers these days have the style and the confidence to shop at both of these places and to

177

mix the clothes into their own, individual outfits. I am targeting a public quite different from the public we targeted with Next back in 1982. My great advantage is that these days I am a known and established figure in the retailing world, and because of my track record, people are more likely to listen to me than to a complete newcomer.

The philosophy of cooperation that I've spoken about will also characterize my relationship with the rest of the GDP staff. When I started Next, I had a dream about a different sort of business, where all the workers were equal and where ridiculous hierarchies were abolished. And in our early days, while we remained a small and tightly-knit team, that dream was a reality, but over the years, as I watched the Next family growing into a stratified corporation, I learned that not everybody wants that equality. The people who have joined me at GDP share my dream, and the atmosphere and excitement in our new offices reminds me of the good old days. I'm happy to report, however, that we are starting out in slightly more salubrious surroundings than that old Kendalls building, and that I am not having to put up with a peeling desk! We are very lucky in that we've been given offices in Asda's Lutterworth headquarters, just a ten-minute drive from Liz's and my Leicestershire home. I think that perhaps in spite of my beliefs, I was too dominant in the past, and I now want to take less of a starring role. The problem with delegation is that it's a pointless exercise if you're passing the tasks and decisions on to the wrong people, but I believe that the team I've now recruited will be strong enough to cope with anything.

Perhaps I have become more selfish in my ambitions. Once I was fired by a desire to create employment on a large scale, but now I want to keep a tight control on GDP's growth. The whole business is geared towards the product, and we want to avoid expending energy on all those peripheral, bureaucratic issues which are such a drain on the resources of most companies, and which come hand in hand with massive expansion. If you think about it, retailing is about two things, buying and selling, and everything else is ancillary to that. Where most retailers go wrong is that they spend 99% of their time on the ancillaries, which seems absurd to me. The essence of the George Davies Partnership is an effective informality. We don't, for example, have a company stationery counter, and we rarely hold meetings, as we all sit together in an open plan office, conferring throughout the course of the day. It's the best possible way to communicate and to get things done, as well as the most enjoyable. I've always been impressed by the ability of the Hong Kong Chinese to get things done without becoming enmeshed in bureaucracy, and there's one incident lodged in my memory which usefully illustrates this point. I had returned for a second visit to an excellent bra factory in Hong Kong, and had arranged a meeting with a Chinese woman I had had discussions with three months previously. As we sat down, she opened her diary on the date of our earlier meeting, and there she had written down everything that we had said that day. It was a simple but effective system, and made a nonsense of the files of copious notes many UK business people burden themselves with.

The core GDP team moved into our new headquarters at the beginning of May. Our first task was to get to know Asda's existing merchandise department on the clothes side, and to assess the staff's strengths and weaknesses. *Fashion Weekly* wrote a damaging and inaccurate piece, in which we were accused of marching into Asda and chopping up their team, but in fact, nothing could have been further from the truth. We were highly sensitive to the feelings of these people, and we had laid careful plans so that they should be informed before the press. Sadly, *The Independent* saw fit to leak the news that I would be taking over Asda's clothing department, the day before I was due to go and speak to the Asda staff. Naturally, the piece caused a lot of pain and anxiety to people who had no idea what was going on, and who feared for their future. Sometimes the press doesn't realize the unnecessary misery it can cause. Over the months there has been a natural fall-out of the original Asda staff, some of whom preferred to opt for redundancy money or early retirement, and others of whom simply did not fit in to the new team for one reason or another. It was always our intention, however, to recruit first of all from the Asda ranks, and many of their staff have now become successful members of our team. These transitions need to be handled with real sensitivity, and perhaps my experiences at Next have helped me see that more closely than ever before.

We launch Asda's new clothing range in February 1990. A lot of people have asked me if it's going to be another Next, and my answer has always been 'No'. For a start, we are launching ourselves on a market that has been transformed by the Next revolution, and which is consequently looking for something quite new. But beyond that is my own impulse to do something different, to write another tune rather than a simple variation on the old one. I don't intend to give much away at this stage, but I will say that the ranges, (which include ladies', men's and children's wear, as well as jewellery, shoes, underwear and hosiery), will be launched under a new name that has never been seen before.

Once the concept is up and running, we have plans to launch an upmarket designer range of our own, independently of Asda of course. At the moment property prices are too high, and I am not prepared to take on the overheads my own chain of shops would incur. A way forward might be to team up with somebody who has the shops and doesn't know what to do with them; there are many companies who are currently in the position of having too many unused sites. Different people have different skills, and mine lie in the retailing rather than the property aspects of the business. Eventually I see no reason why we shouldn't have a number of different clients, much in the way an advertising agency does, providing for each an original label and look. We have already had many approaches, including one from a Japanese company which is interested in our producing a British range for them.

Life has a peculiar way of working out in the end. Ten days after my firing, I received a letter from a psychic who claimed that she could 'read' my future in my face. At the time, I was so confused and shocked that I couldn't see where I was going, but now it is easy to note the accuracy of this complete stranger's assessments and predictions. The following are extracts from her letter:

'What has happened to you was meant to happen. You are a Chief, not an Indian and should NOT be an employee. Recent events are the way of making you see the path you must follow. You are very hard working, with a vivid imagination, and impatient when others fail to see what you see. You MUST start your own company (don't consider any offers of employment, however attractive), but not until later in the year. . . . The day will come, I promise

you, when you will thank fate for what has happened to you now. You will run a very successful, though smaller, company over which you have total control. I know how painful these happenings are, but we survive, very much wiser and go on to much better things. . . . You CAN and WILL be successful, get out there and show 'em!'

Next might have been a major chapter in my business life, but it was by no means the final one. From where I stand now, I see it as a stepping stone which has helped me to get to where I really want to be. Although many people might have thought otherwise, Next was never mine, and as employee I was never a true entrepreneur. Now that I am running my own company, I feel that I am at last free to operate according to my own vision and principles.

I have learned many lessons from the Next experience, but getting to know myself and my priorities in life has been the most important one. The end of Next is just the beginning of a new chapter. Someone said to me the other day that I couldn't possibly be as excited about GDP as I had been when I started Next, and I replied, 'You must be joking, of course I am. I'm even more excited, because this is going to be better!' Which reminds me of something my sister, Pamela, said to me years ago: 'Your trouble, George, is that you genuinely believe that wherever *you* happen to be at the time is the best place to be.' And it's an accurate description. Perhaps that's why I've always had the determination to bounce back.